Academic Learning Series:

# Network+ Certification, Fourth Edition

Lab Manual

*Craig Zacker*

PUBLISHED BY
Microsoft Press
A Division of Microsoft Corporation
One Microsoft Way
Redmond, Washington 98052-6399

Library of Congress Control Number 2005935315

Printed and bound in the United States of America.

1 2 3 4 5 6 7 8 9    QWT    9 8 7 6 5

Distributed in Canada by H.B. Fenn and Company Ltd.

A CIP catalogue record for this book is available from the British Library.

Microsoft Press books are available through booksellers and distributors worldwide. For further information about international editions, contact your local Microsoft Corporation office or contact Microsoft Press International directly at fax (425) 936-7329. Visit our Web site at www.microsoft.com/learning/. Send comments to *moac@microsoft.com*.

Microsoft, Active Directory, MS-DOS, PowerPoint, Windows, Windows NT, and Windows Server are either registered trademarks or trademarks of Microsoft Corporation in the United States and/or other countries.

The example companies, organizations, products, domain names, e-mail addresses, logos, people, places, and events depicted herein are fictitious. No association with any real company, organization, product, domain name, e-mail address, logo, person, place, or event is intended or should be inferred.

This book expresses the author's views and opinions. The information contained in this book is provided without any express, statutory, or implied warranties. Neither the authors, Microsoft Corporation, nor its resellers, or distributors will be held liable for any damages caused or alleged to be caused either directly or indirectly by this book.

**Acquisitions Editor:** Lori Oviatt
**Project Editor:** Laura Sackerman

SubAssy Part No. X11-77545
Body Part No. X11-77546

# CONTENTS

## LAB 1
# USING NETWORK MONITOR

**This lab contains the following exercises and activities:**

- Exercise 1-1: Installing Network Monitor

- Exercise 1-2: Configuring Network Monitor

- Exercise 1-3: Capturing Traffic

- Exercise 1-4: Analyzing a Frame

- Exercise 1-5: Using Display Filters

- Lab Review Questions

- Lab Challenge 1-1: Using Capture Filters

- Lab Challenge 1-2: Capturing FTP Traffic

## BEFORE YOU BEGIN

This lab introduces you to the Network Monitor application included with Windows Server 2003. Network Monitor is a protocol analyzer—an application that can capture network frames and display their contents. You will use Network Monitor in the labs throughout this course to examine network traffic.

Before you begin this lab, you might want to look at the "Protocol Analyzers" section in Chapter 11 of the textbook to familiarize yourself with the basic functions of a protocol analyzer.

To start this lab, you will need to obtain the following information from your instructor:

- The two-digit number assigned to your lab group. This number is used in the name of your lab domain (LG*xx*, where *xx* is the number assigned to your group).

**After completing this lab, you will be able to:**

- Install Network Monitor on a computer running Microsoft Windows Server 2003.
- Configure Network Monitor.
- Capture and view network traffic.
- Understand the data encapsulation process by viewing the protocols at the various layers of the Open Systems Interconnection (OSI) reference model.
- Customize a display filter.

**Estimated lesson time:   135 minutes**

## SCENARIO

You are the new network administrator for Contoso, Ltd. The network has multiple servers running Windows Server 2003 and workstations running Microsoft Windows XP and Microsoft Windows 2000. During your first week on the job many users have mentioned how network performance has been degrading in recent months. However, the previous administrator left you no documentation about the network installation or configuration, so you must start the process of documenting and troubleshooting the network from scratch.

You decide to first examine the network traffic in detail over the course of several days. To do this, you will install the Network Monitor application that is included with Windows Server 2003 and perform a detailed analysis of protocols running on the network, starting from the bottom of the OSI reference model and working your way up.

In this lab, you will install Network Monitor for the first time and learn how to use its basic functions.

## EXERCISE 1-1: INSTALLING NETWORK MONITOR

**Estimated completion time: 15 minutes**

In this exercise you will install Network Monitor on Computer*xx* so you can capture and analyze network traffic samples throughout this course.

1. Log on to Computer*xx* as Administrator, using the password **Pa$$w0rd**.

2. Click Start, select All Programs, select Accessories, and then select Command Prompt.

   The Command Prompt window appears.

**3.** In the Command Prompt window, type **ipconfig /all** and then press
ENTER.

Based on the Ipconfig information displayed in the Command Prompt
window, answer the following questions:

> **QUESTION**   What Internet Protocol (IP) address is your computer
> using?

> **QUESTION**   How did the computer obtain this IP address? How can
> you tell?

> **QUESTION**   What is the physical address assigned to the Ethernet
> network interface adapter installed in the computer?

> **QUESTION**   What does the Physical Address value represent?

**4.** Type **exit** in the Command Prompt window, and then press ENTER.

The Command Prompt window closes.

**5.** Click Start, select Control Panel, and then select Add Or Remove
Programs.

The Add Or Remove Programs dialog box appears.

**6.** Click Add/Remove Windows Components.

The Windows Components Wizard launches.

**7.** Scroll down in the Components list, select Management And Monitoring Tools, and then click Details.

The Management And Monitoring Tools dialog box appears.

**8.** Select the Network Monitor Tools check box, and then click OK to
close the dialog box.

9. Click Next.

10. The Configuring Components page appears as the wizard begins to copy the appropriate files. After a short delay, an Insert Disk message box appears, instructing you to insert the Windows Server 2003 installation CD- ROM into the drive. Click OK to display the Files Needed dialog box.

11. Type **c:\win2k3\i386** in the Copy Files From text box, and then click OK.

    The wizard continues copying files.

12. Click Finish to close the wizard and complete the installation.

13. Close the Add Or Remove Programs dialog box.

## EXERCISE 1-2: CONFIGURING NETWORK MONITOR

**Estimated completion time: 15 minutes**
In this exercise, you will run Network Monitor for the first time and configure some of its settings.

1. On Computer*xx*, click Start, select Administrative Tools, and then select Network Monitor.

   A Network Monitor window opens and a message box appears, instructing you to specify the network from which you want to capture data. Network Monitor will capture all of the frames sent to or from the network that you choose.

2. Click OK to close the message box.

   The Select A Network dialog box appears.

3. Expand the Local Computer heading, and then, in the left pane, select the Local Area Connection interface that displays a MAC address value in the right pane that matches the Physical Address value you wrote down in Exercise 1-1.

**NOTE   Physical Address Notation**   The physical (or MAC) address of the network interface adapter is in hexadecimal form. The Ipconfig display shows dashes between the bytes of the address, while the Select A Network dialog box does not.

4. Click OK.

   The Local Area Connection Capture window appears. The title bar of this window shows the system name of the network interface adapter you just selected (Local Area Connection).

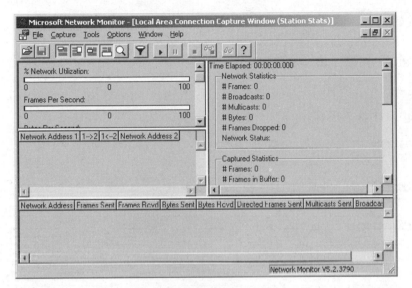

5. From the Capture menu, select Buffer Settings.

   The Capture Buffer Settings dialog box appears.

6. Change the Buffer Size (MB) setting from 1 (its default value) to 10, and then click OK.

   The capture buffer is an area of the hard disk where Network Monitor temporarily saves the frames it captures from the network. By default, the capture buffer is only 1 MB, but you have just increased it to 10 MB, enabling you to capture more frames at one time. You can increase the size of the capture buffer as needed, as long as you have sufficient disk space on the drive.

7. From the Capture menu, select Addresses.

   The Address Database dialog box appears. The address database contains the addresses read from captured frames and their equivalent names, when available.

**QUESTION**  Which data-link layer protocols does Network Monitor support? How can you tell?

**QUESTION**  What are the Name, Address, and Type values for the entries without asterisks (*)?

**QUESTION**  The entries with asterisks represent the broadcast and multicast addresses that Network Monitor recognizes by default. What do the entries without asterisks represent?

8.  Select the LOCAL entry with the network interface adapter's physical address, and then click Edit.

    The Address Information dialog box appears.

9.  In the Name text box, replace LOCAL with the name of the computer (**Computer*xx***, where *xx* is the number assigned to the computer).

10.  Select the Permanent Name check box, and then click OK.

**QUESTION**  How has the entry changed?

**QUESTION**  How can changing the names associated with computer addresses help you?

11.  Click Save.

    The Save Addresses As dialog box appears.

12.  Type *Addresses* in the File Name text box, and then click Save.

    The address database entries you modified are saved as the filename you specified, with an .adr extension, and are located in the C:\Documents And Settings\Administrator\My Documents\My Captures folder.

13.  Click Close to close the Address Database dialog box.

14.  From the File menu, select Exit.

    Network Monitor closes.

The physical (or MAC) address of the network interface adapter is in hexadecimal form. The Ipconfig display shows dashes between the bytes of the address, while the Select A Network dialog box does not.

# EXERCISE 1-3: CAPTURING TRAFFIC

**Estimated completion time: 15 minutes**

In this exercise, you will use Network Monitor to capture and examine network traffic.

1. Click Start, select Administrative Tools, and then select Network Monitor.

   Network Monitor opens, displaying the Capture Window you saw in Exercise 1-2.

2. From the Capture menu, select Addresses.

   The Address Database dialog box appears.

3. Click Load.

   The Open Address File dialog box appears.

4. Select the address file you created in Exercise 1-2, and then click Open.

5. Click Close to close the Address Database dialog box.

   > **NOTE** **Using Saved Address Information** To use your saved address information, you must open your address file each time you launch Network Monitor. If you change address database information during a Network Monitor session, you must save your changes to your address file before exiting the application.

6. From the Capture menu, select Start.

   Network Monitor begins capturing data.

   > **NOTE** **Starting a Capture** To start the capture, you can also click the Start Capture icon on the toolbar or press F10.

7. Wait for about two or three minutes, and then, from the Capture menu, select Stop. (If you don't see any network activity, you might need to wait longer.)

   > **NOTE** **Stopping a Capture** To stop a capture, you can also click the Stop Capture icon on the toolbar or press F11.

8. Using the information displayed in the Local Area Connection Capture Window, answer the following questions:

**QUESTION**   How many frames did Network Monitor capture?

**QUESTION**   How many bytes of data did Network Monitor capture?

**QUESTION**   Why was so little data captured?

**QUESTION**   What was the destination for most (if not all) of the frames you captured?

9.  Start a new capture, and answer No when Network Monitor asks if you want to save the previous capture.

10. Click Start, select All Programs, select Accessories, and then select Command Prompt.

    A Command Prompt window appears.

11. Type **copy \\server01\windist\eula.txt c:\win2k3\i386 /y** and press ENTER.

    The system copies the Eula.txt file from Server01 to Computer01, overwriting the existing copy.

12. Repeat the copy command a couple more times to generate more network traffic.

13. Return to Network Monitor, and from the Capture menu, select Stop.

**14.** Based on the information shown in the Capture Window, answer the following questions:

> **QUESTION**   How can you tell how many frames were captured to the buffer?

> **QUESTION**   How many frames were captured to the buffer?

> **QUESTION**   How can you tell how much space is left in the buffer?

> **QUESTION**   How much space is left in the capture buffer?

> **QUESTION**   How can you tell the physical address of the Server01 computer?

> **QUESTION**   What is the physical address of the Server01 computer?

> **NOTE   Network Monitor and Hardware Addresses**   Depending on the manufacturer of the network interface adapters in your computers, the hardware addresses displayed in Network Monitor might be 6-byte hexadecimal values or the 3-byte organizationally unique identifiers (OUIs) might be decoded into an abbreviation of the manufacturer's name.

**15.** Right-click the physical address in the Network Address column that represents the Server01 computer, and then select Edit Address *xxxxxxxxxxxx* (where *xxxxxxxxxxxx* is the physical address).

The Address Information dialog box appears.

**16.** Type **Server01** in the Name text box, select the Permanent Name check box, and then click OK.

> **QUESTION**   What happens? Why?

> **QUESTION**   How many bytes have been transmitted by the Server01 computer? How can you tell?

**17.** Leave Network Monitor open for the next exercise.

# EXERCISE 1-4: ANALYZING A FRAME

**Estimated completion time: 20 minutes**

In this exercise, you will look at one of the frames you captured in the previous exercise and analyze its contents.

1.  In Network Monitor, from the Capture menu, select Display Captured Data.

    > **NOTE  Displaying Captured Data**   To display the data you have already captured, you can also click the Display Captured Data icon on the toolbar or press F12. When a capture is running, you can also stop the capture process and display the captured data in one step by selecting Stop And View from the Capture menu, or by clicking the Stop And View Capture button, or by pressing SHIFT+F11.

2.  The Capture: # (Summary) window appears, where # is the number of the capture in the current Network Monitor session, containing the data you captured in Exercise 1-3.

3.  Scroll down in the Capture: # (Summary) window until you see frames mentioning the Eula.txt file name in the Description column.

4.  Scroll down in the Capture: # (Summary) window and select the next frame that contains the values shown in the following table:

| Src MAC Addr | Dst MAC Addr | Protocol | Description |
| --- | --- | --- | --- |
| Server01 | Computerxx | NBT | SS Session Message Cont. |

This frame contains part of the Eula.txt file you copied from Server01 to your computer while Network Monitor was capturing frames.

> **QUESTION**   What is the size of the message contained in the frame you selected (as specified in the Description column)?

**5.** Double-click the frame you selected.

The window splits into three panes (or segments), as follows:

❑ *Summary pane*–Contains the frame listing you were just viewing

❑ *Detail pane*–Contains the interpreted contents of the frame

❑ *Hex pane*–Contains the raw contents of the frame, in both hexadecimal and ASCII formats

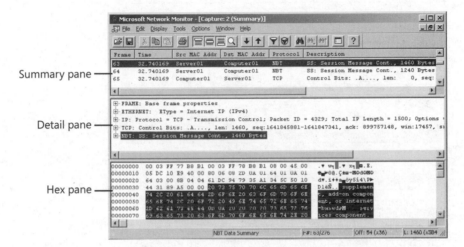

**6.** Take a screen shot (using ALT+PRNT SCRN) of the entire Microsoft Network Monitor window, and then paste it into a WordPad document named LGxxLab01-1.rtf (where xx is the assigned number of your group) on your host computer.

Your instructor will ask you to turn the file in at the end of the lab.

**7.** Adjust the borders between the panes to enlarge the Detail pane.

**8.** Click the plus sign (+) next to the FRAME: Base Frame Properties entry in the Detail pane.

The FRAME: Base Frame Properties entry is expanded. This pane contains general information about the captured frame.

> **QUESTION**  What is the total length of the frame you selected?

> **QUESTION**  How many bytes of the frame are added during the data encapsulation process? How can you tell?

**9.** Select the ETHERNET entry in the Detail pane.

Notice that selecting the ETHERNET entry in the Detail pane also causes the bytes corresponding to the Ethernet header to be selected in the Hex pane.

**QUESTION**   What are the values of the first 6 bytes in the selected area of the Hex pane?

**NOTE   Reading Hex**   Remember that in hexadecimal notation, each byte is represented by two characters, so 6 bytes worth of data is expressed as six 2-character strings.

10. Expand the ETHERNET entry in the Detail pane.

Network Monitor displays the contents of the Ethernet header fields.

**QUESTION**   What is the value of the Destination Address field in the Ethernet header?

**QUESTION**   How does this value compare with the first 6 bytes of raw data from the Hex pane you recorded earlier?

11. Select the IP entry in the Detail pane.

Notice that the Hex pane display changes to select the raw data that makes up the IP header fields.

**QUESTION**   As you move down past FRAME in the Detail pane entries, you move higher in the OSI reference model, with each successive entry representing a different protocol. For each of the following OSI model layers, specify what protocol is operating in the frame you are currently analyzing.

1. Data-link
2. Network

3. Transport

4. Application

**NOTE  Protocols and Encapsulation**   Not all frames have only a single protocol operating at a given OSI model layer, as in this example. In some cases two or more protocols are operating at the same layer. The use of multiple protocols at the same layer in one frame is most common in the application layer, but it can occur in the network layer as well.

**QUESTION**   What protocol provides the outermost header in the frame you are currently analyzing? How can you tell?

**NOTE  Analyzing Individual Protocols**   You will learn more about analyzing the functions of the individual protocols in a frame in later labs.

12. Select the NBT entry in the Detail pane.

The NBT message data is highlighted in the Hex pane.

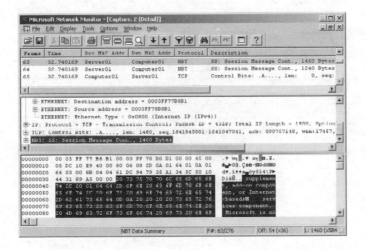

**QUESTION**   Why does the NBT message data appear in the Hex pane as clear, readable text, while the data generated by the other protocols does not?

13. From the File menu, select Save As.

The Save As dialog box appears.

14. Type **lab1** in the File Name text box, and then click Save.

Network Monitor copies the contents of the capture buffer to the Lab1.cap file in the C:\Documents and Settings\Administrator\My Documents\My Captures folder.

15. Leave the Network Monitor window open for the next exercise.

## EXERCISE 1-5: USING DISPLAY FILTERS

**Estimated completion time: 15 minutes**

In this exercise, you will use a display filter to control the information that Network Monitor displays. In many cases Network Monitor captures different types of frames, and display filters help you zero in on exactly the frames you want to study.

1. On Computerxx, in Network Monitor, double-click any entry in the Summary pane to return to a single-paned capture summary display.

2. From the Display menu, select Filter.

The Display Filter dialog box appears.

3. Select the ANY <--> ANY entry, and then click Edit Expression.

The Expression dialog box appears.

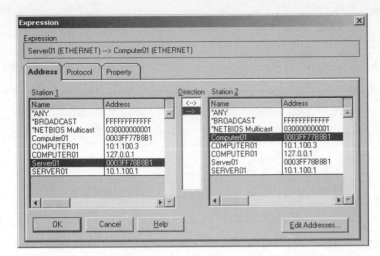

4. In the Station 1 list, select one of the Server01 entries.

5. In the Station 2 list, select one of the Computer*xx* entries (but not the one with the 127.0.0.1 loopback address).

6. In the Direction list, select the right- pointing arrow (–>) entry, and then click OK.

   Your filter selections appear in the Display Filter dialog box.

7. Click OK to close the Display Filter dialog box.

   **QUESTION**   What happens?

8. Open the Display Filter dialog box again, select the Protocol == Any entry, and then click Edit Expression.

   The Expression dialog box appears.

9. Click Disable All.

   All of the protocols listed in the Enabled Protocols list are moved to the Disabled Protocols list.

10. Scroll down in the Disabled Protocols list, select the NBT entry, and then click Enable.

    The NBT protocol is moved to the Enabled Protocols list.

11. Click OK to close the Expression dialog box, and then click OK to close the Display Filter dialog box.

    **QUESTION**   What happens?

**QUESTION**  Why do other frames, such as those with SMB in the Protocol column, still appear if the display filter is configured to show only NBT frames?

12. Take a screen shot (ALT+PRNT SCRN) of the Microsoft Network Monitor window, making sure that the display filter you created is applied. Then paste it into a WordPad document named LGxxLab01-2.rtf (where *xx* is the assigned number of your group) to turn in at the end of the lab.

13. From the Display menu, select Disable Filter.

**QUESTION**  What happens?

When you apply a display filter to a capture, the frames that are being filtered out are still present in the capture file; creating a filter just prevents them from appearing in the display.

14. From the File menu, select Exit to close Network Monitor.

   When prompted, save your address database to the same file name you specified in Exercise 1-2.

## LAB REVIEW QUESTIONS

**Estimated completion time: 20 minutes**

1. Your first attempt to capture traffic using Network Monitor resulted in only a few frames in the buffer. Why was this the case when other groups in the classroom were likely performing the same activity as you at the same time?

2. If, during Exercise 1-3, you captured the frames generated while copying Winnt.exe instead of Eula.txt, how would the NBT message data you analyzed in Exercise 1-4 be different?

3. To troubleshoot a problem on a computer running Windows Server 2003, you want to capture a network traffic sample over a long period of time using the Windows Server 2003 version of Network Monitor. However, the computer experiencing the problem is seriously short on disk space. Which of the following options will let you perform the capture you need? Explain your answer.

   a. Increase the size of the capture buffer

   b. Create a display filter

   c. Create a capture filter

   d. Run Network Monitor on a different computer

4. Why is it that the values of the Ethernet addresses in the Detail pane of a frame capture are identical to the corresponding Ethernet data specified in the Hex pane, but the values of the IP header fields in the Detail pane are different from the corresponding Hex pane data?

## LAB CHALLENGE 1-1: USING CAPTURE FILTERS

**Estimated completion time: 15 minutes**

In Exercise 1-5 you learned how to use display filters to isolate specific frames in a network traffic sample that has already been captured. Capture filters work in much the same way, except that you use them to control which frames Network Monitor saves to the buffer during a capture. You create capture filters from the Local Area Connection Capture window instead of the Capture: # (Summary) window. To complete this lab challenge, perform the following activities:

1. Create a filter that will restrict a capture to frames that use the IP protocol and that are transmitted by your computer (Computerxx) to the Server01 computer.

2. Take a screen shot (ALT+PRNT SCRN) of the Capture Filter dialog box containing the properly configured filter expressions, and then paste it into a WordPad document named LGxxLab01-3.rtf (where xx is the assigned number of your group) to turn in at the end of the lab.

3. Start a capture, using the filter, and repeat step 11 from Exercise 1-3, where you copy Eula.txt from Server01 to Computerxx. Then take a screen shot of the Capture: # (Summary) window that contains the frames you captured with the filter and paste it into a WordPad document named LGxxLab01-4.rtf to turn in at the end of the lab.

4. Close Network Monitor when you are finished.

## LAB CHALLENGE 1-2: CAPTURING FTP TRAFFIC

**Estimated completion time: 20 minutes**

The version of Network Monitor included with Windows Server 2003 can capture and display any traffic sent or received by the computer on which it is running. This can include traffic containing sensitive information. For example, when an application transmits user names and passwords in clear text (that is, unencrypted form), Network Monitor can display those names and passwords. File Transfer Protocol (FTP) is just such an application.

To complete this lab challenge, follow these steps:

1.  Configure Network Monitor to capture traffic as you connect to the FTP server service on the Server01 computer.

2.  Log on with the user name **anonymous** and type **hello** for the password.

3.  Locate the captured frame containing the password you supplied and display it in Network Monitor's Hex pane.

4.  Take a screen shot (ALT+PRNT SCRN) of the Network Monitor window and paste it into a WordPad document named LGxxLab01-5.rtf (where xx is the assigned number of your group) to turn in at the end of the lab.

5.  Close Network Monitor without saving the captured packets.

## LAB 2
# UNDERSTANDING NETWORK COMPONENTS

**This lab contains the following exercises and activities:**

■ Exercise 2-1: Examining a Cable

■ Exercise 2-2: Recognizing Cable Faults

■ Exercise 2-3: Examining a Network Interface Adapter

■ Exercise 2-4: Examining a Hub

■ Exercise 2-5: Documenting a Network

■ Lab Review Questions

■ Lab Challenge 2-1: Using Connectivity Devices

## BEFORE YOU BEGIN

Before you begin this lab, you will need to get the following materials from your instructor:

■ A UTP demonstration cable

■ An Ethernet network interface adapter card, along with its documentation

■ A stand-alone Ethernet hub or switch, along with its documentation

> **NOTE**  If you don't have a demonstration UTP cable, Ethernet network interface card adapter, or Ethernet hub, you can examine the photographs in this lab.

**After completing this lab, you will be able to:**

■ Understand the construction of an unshielded twisted pair (UTP) cable.

■ Identify common UTP wiring faults.

■ Identify the connectors on an Ethernet network interface adapter card.

■ Specify the functions of the connectors on an Ethernet hub.

■ Identify the functions of the light-emitting diodes (LEDs) on Ethernet hubs and network interface adapter cards.

**Estimated lesson time:    130 minutes**

## SCENARIO

You are a network administrator who worked for several years at a company that used Token Ring networks exclusively. You were recently hired by a new company that uses Ethernet, and this is your first exposure to Ethernet equipment. You want to carefully study Ethernet cables, network interface adapters, and hubs before beginning your new job.

## EXERCISE 2-1: EXAMINING A CABLE

**Estimated completion time: 20 minutes**

1.  Take the demonstration cable provided by your instructor and examine the wires inside the sheath at the cut end. If you don't have a demonstration cable, examine the following photograph.

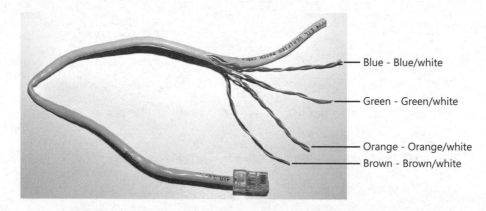

Blue - Blue/white

Green - Green/white

Orange - Orange/white
Brown - Brown/white

**QUESTION**    *How many wires are inside the cable sheath?*

**2.** Notice the colors of the wires inside the cable. Each twisted pair consists of one solid colored wire (brown, blue, green, or orange) and one wire of the same color with a white stripe.

> **NOTE   Naming Wire Colors**   For the purposes of this lab, the second wire in a pair will be referred to by the color of the first wire plus white, as in "green/white."

**3.** Notice that each of the wire pairs in the cable is twisted using a different number of twists per inch.

> **QUESTION**   What is the color of the wire pair with the greatest number of twists per inch?   *orange/white*

> **QUESTION**   Why do the wire pairs have different twist rates?

**4.** Now examine the other end of the cable, where the wires enter the connector. Hold the cable with the connector pointing to the left and the connector's metal contacts facing down away from you. The connector's plastic locking tab should be pointing up toward you. Look down into the connector and list the colors of the wires in order from top to bottom, numbering them from 1 to 8.

Orange/white
Orange
Green/white
Blue
Blue/white
Green
Brown/white
Brown

**5.** Consult the diagrams of the three most common RJ-45 pinout standards in the following illustration and compare them to your cable.

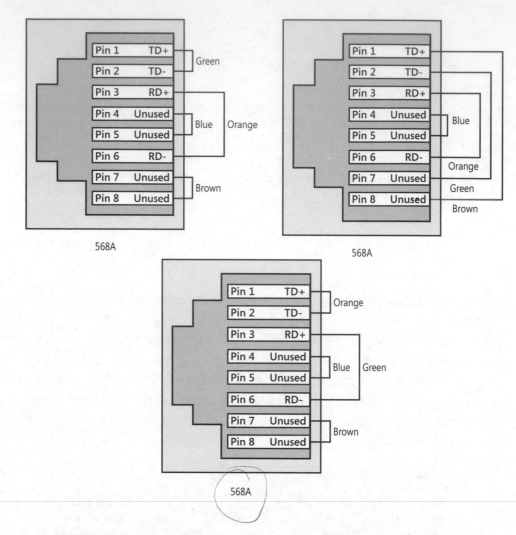

**NOTE**   **Reviewing Wiring Standards**   You might want to review the section titled "Wiring Standards" in Chapter 2 of your textbook.

**QUESTION**   Which of the RJ-45 pinout standards is your cable using?

**QUESTION**   Can your cable be used on an Ethernet network? Why or why not?

6. Compare your cable (or the photograph shown in step 4) with the diagram of RJ-45 pin functions shown in the following illustration.

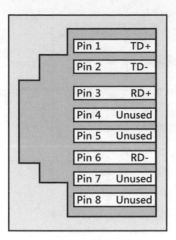

**QUESTION**   What colors are the two wires that function as the transmit pair in your cable?

**QUESTION**   What colors are the two wires that function as the receive pair?

# EXERCISE 2-2: RECOGNIZING CABLE FAULTS

### Estimated completion time: 15 minutes

Bulk cable installations have the potential for many types of errors that can affect network communications. When installing cables to wall plates and patch panels or when attaching RJ-45 connectors, you must make sure that each wire is connected individually to the correct pins at both ends of the connection. Some of the types of installation wiring faults are covered in the section titled "Network Testing and Monitoring Tools" in Chapter 11 of your textbook. Study that section and then, for each of the following diagrams, specify the type of wiring fault it illustrates, if any.

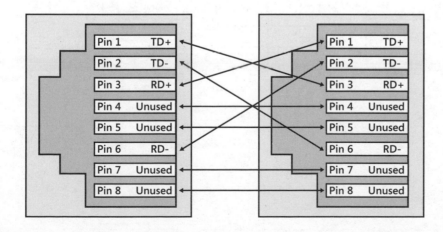

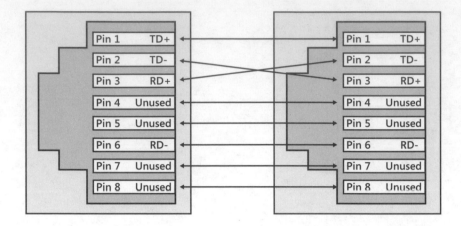

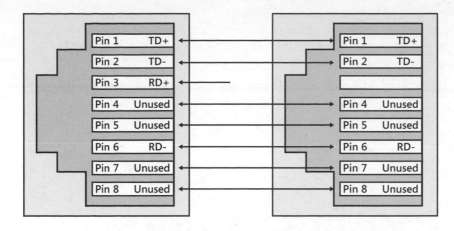

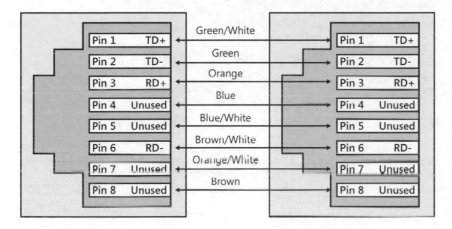

# EXERCISE 2-3: EXAMINING A NETWORK INTERFACE ADAPTER

**Estimated completion time: 15 minutes**

Your instructor will give you a network interface adapter card and its documentation. In Lab 3, you will install the card into one of your lab group computers. Before installing the card, however, examine it and take note of its features and construction. You might also need to consult the card's documentation to answer some of the questions in this lab. If you don't have a demonstration network interface adapter card, examine the photographs.

> **NOTE**   *Before Handling a Network Interface Adapter Card*   The network interface adapter card you receive from your instructor should be kept in an antistatic bag whenever you aren't examining or installing it. When handling the card, grab it by the metal slot cover and avoid touching the electronic components or the connectors. Your instructor might give you an antistatic wrist strap or mat and explain how to use it. This is to prevent

static electricity from damaging the card. If you don't have a wrist strap or mat, be sure to ground yourself by touching the metal part of a computer case or other grounded metal object before removing the card from its bag.

1. Take the network interface adapter card out of its bag and put it on the desk with the components on the card facing up.

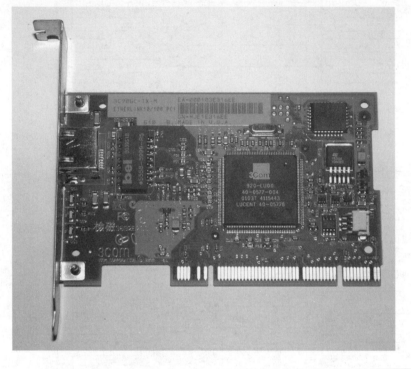

**QUESTION**    What type of bus connector does the network interface adapter card have?

2. Look at the slot cover, which will be visible when the card is installed in the computer.

**QUESTION**   How many cable connectors are on your network interface adapter card, and what types are they?

**QUESTION**   How many LEDs are on your network interface adapter card?

**QUESTION**   What functions do the LEDs perform?

**QUESTION**   At what speeds can your network interface adapter card operate?

3.  Replace the adapter card in its protective bag.

# EXERCISE 2-4: EXAMINING A HUB

**Estimated completion time: 10 minutes**

Your instructor will give you an Ethernet hub or switch and the documentation to go with it. You will use the hub or switch in Lab 3 to build your own lab group network. If you don't have a demonstration hub, examine the photographs.

Take the hub out of its box or bag and examine it from all sides.

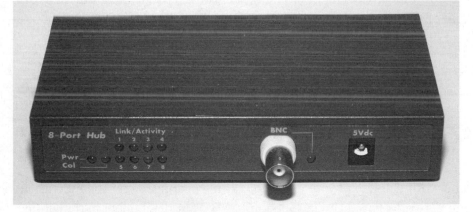

**QUESTION**   What is the total number of RJ-45 ports in your hub?

**QUESTION**   How many of the RJ-45 ports can you use to connect computers to the hub?

**QUESTION**   What must you do to connect your hub to a standard computer port in another hub?

**QUESTION**   How many LEDs are on the hub?

**QUESTION**   What are the functions of the LEDs?

Return the hub to its box or bag.

# EXERCISE 2-5: DOCUMENTING A NETWORK

### Estimated completion time: 15 minutes

In this exercise you practice documenting a network by drawing a diagram of the equipment in your classroom. In Lab 3 you will install a second network interface adapter into your Computerxx computer and connect it to your Computeryy, using the hub you have been given. This will create a separate lab group network consisting of your two computers. The original network interface adapter in Computerxx is connected to the classroom network.

**NOTE   Classroom Network Architecture**   For the purposes of this lab, assume that the jacks for the classroom network are cabled to a single large hub. The two classroom servers (named Server01 and LinuxServer01) and the Computerxx computer in each student lab group are connected to this hub.

Draw a network diagram of your classroom as it will appear after the individual lab group networks have been installed in Lab 3. Your diagram should include the classroom hub, the classroom servers, all of the lab group computers, the lab group hubs, and all the cables that connect them together. Be sure to label each computer and hub.

# LAB REVIEW QUESTIONS

### Estimated completion time: 25 minutes

1.  If all the computers on your classroom network use cables conforming to the 568A pinout standard, what will happen if you connect a new computer using a 568B cable? Explain your answer.

2. If all the computers on your classroom network use cables conforming to the 568A pinout standard, what will happen if you connect a new computer using a USOC cable?

3. What would happen if the wire pairs in a network cable were not twisted at all but ran straight through from connector to connector?

4. Standard network cables are wired straight through, with each pin in one connector wired to the corresponding pin in the other connector. Based on the photograph shown in Exercise 2-1 and the wire color order you specified in step 4 of that exercise, what is the color order on the other connector for a crossover cable?

5. Which of the cable faults illustrated in Exercise 2-2 would not be detected by a standard wire map tester?

6. Why do some Ethernet network interface adapters have BNC connectors in addition to RJ-45 ports but Ethernet hubs do not?

7. In your diagram of your classroom network, which devices are functioning as routers?

## LAB CHALLENGE 2-1: USING CONNECTIVITY DEVICES

**Estimated completion time: 30 minutes**

In Exercise 2-5 you created a network diagram of your classroom, which consists of multiple lab group networks connected to the classroom network by computers functioning as routers. For the purposes of this challenge, assume that each lab group network in the classroom consists of 10 computers instead of just two, and explain how each of the following equipment changes would affect network traffic in the classroom. Your explanations should specify how collision domains and broadcast domains are affected and what types of traffic (internetwork or intranetwork) would be affected and how.

1. Replace all hubs with switches.

2. Replace all routers with bridges.

3. Replace the classroom hub with a switch.

4. Replace all routers with switches.

5. Replace all routers and hubs with switches.

## LAB 3
# BUILDING A NETWORK

**This lab contains the following exercises and activities:**

■ Exercise 3-1: Installing a Network Interface Adapter

■ Exercise 3-2: Viewing Network Interface Adapter Hardware Resources in Windows

■ Exercise 3-3: Configuring Hardware Resources in Windows Manually

■ Exercise 3-4: Building a LAN

■ Exercise 3-5: Testing LAN Communications

■ Lab Review Questions

■ Lab Challenge 3-1: Configuring Hardware Resources in Linux

## BEFORE YOU BEGIN

To complete this lab, you will need to get the following materials from your instructor:

■ An Ethernet network interface adapter card.

■ A standalone Ethernet hub.

■ Two Category 5 (CAT5) unshielded twisted-pair (UTP) cables.

■ An antistatic wrist strap or pad (optional).

■ Tools for opening the computer case (if needed).

■ The two-digit number assigned to your lab group. This number is used in the name of your lab group (LG*xx*, where *xx* is the number assigned to your group).

> **IMPORTANT** To complete Lab Challenge 3-1, you must have access to a computer with Linux installed on it. Check with your instructor before beginning Lab Challenge 3-1.

**After completing this lab, you will be able to:**

- Install a network interface adapter card in a computer.
- Install and configure hardware in a computer running Microsoft Windows.
- Construct a simple Ethernet local area network (LAN).
- Test LAN communications.

**Estimated lesson time:   130 minutes**

# SCENARIO

You are the network administrator for Lucerne Publishing, a small business that has recently acquired one of its competitors, Litware, Inc. You need to connect Litware's six-node network into the Lucerne network, but no budget is available for a new router. You do have an extra network interface adapter card, however, and you plan to install it into one of your existing computers that's running Microsoft Windows Server 2003 so that you can connect the computer to both networks. You will configure the computer to function as a router later.

# EXERCISE 3-1: INSTALLING A NETWORK INTERFACE ADAPTER

**Estimated completion time: 20 minutes**

In this exercise you will install the network interface adapter card into Computer*xx*.

> **IMPORTANT**   Check with your instructor before starting this exercise or opening up your host computer. Your instructor might supply you with a separate computer in which you can install a network interface adapter or have you just examine the photographs in this exercise.

1. Shut down Computer*xx* (if it is running) and unplug the power cable from the back of the case.

2. Prepare your work area by setting up the antistatic equipment you have been provided.

> **IMPORTANT**   Protecting Your Computer and Yourself   Working inside a computer can be hazardous, both to you and to the computer. Static electricity can damage many of the components inside a computer, so be sure to ground yourself before opening the case and touching anything inside. You can ground yourself by using an antistatic wriststrap or an antistatic mat or just by touching a

*grounded metal object before working on the computer. To protect yourself from electric shock, always remember to unplug a computer from its power source before opening up the case.*

3. Remove the cover from the computer case and set it aside.

Most modern computers use thumbscrews, plastic latches, or a combination of the two to hold the cover onto the computer. On older machines you might have to remove a number of Phillips or Torx head screws to open the case.

4. Locate the computer's expansion bus and answer the following questions.

**QUESTION**   How many expansion slots are in the computer?

**QUESTION**   How many of the expansion slots in the computer are unoccupied?

**QUESTION**   What types of slots are they?

5. Locate an appropriate bus slot for the network interface adapter card.

In most cases your card will require a PCI slot. If no slots of the appropriate type are free in your computer, notify the instructor before proceeding.

**6.** Remove the protective cover from the slot.

**7.** Remove the network interface adapter card from its antistatic bag and hold it over the slot you selected.

**8.** Line up the bus connector on the card with the bus slot in the computer.

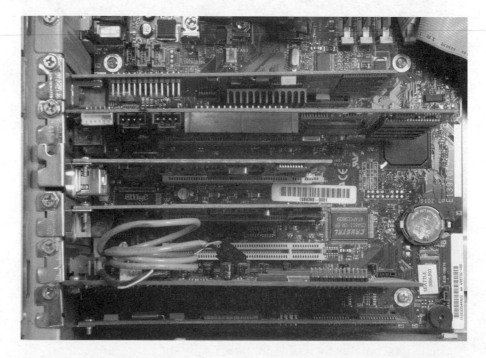

9. Push down firmly on the top edge of the card to seat it fully into the slot.

Different types of cards require slightly different techniques to get them into a slot. The bus connectors on ISA cards typically have rounded corners, allowing you to push the entire connector down into the slot at once. PCI cards typically have sharper corners, so it is easier to hold the card at a slight angle and push one end of the connector into the slot first, and then the other end.

> **IMPORTANT**  *Be Careful*   If you have problems getting the card into the slot, ask your instructor for help. An expansion card requires firm pressure to seat it completely into the slot, but pushing down too firmly can damage the card or even crack the computer's motherboard.

10. Secure the card in the slot, using the screw or other mechanism.

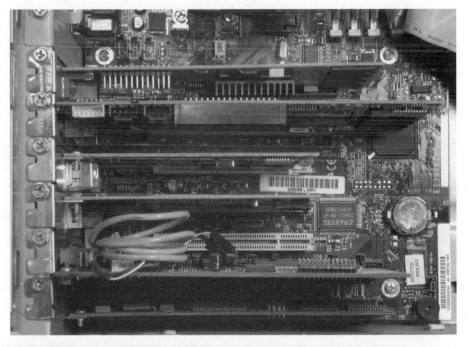

Save the slot cover that the card replaced and return it to your instructor.

11. Replace the cover on the computer case and secure it in place.

12. Reconnect the power cable to the computer.

## EXERCISE 3-2: VIEWING NETWORK INTERFACE ADAPTER HARDWARE RESOURCES IN WINDOWS

**Estimated completion time: 15 minutes**

In this exercise you will use the Windows Device Manager console and the Ipconfig.exe utility to view the hardware resources that the network interface adapters in Computer*xx* are using.

1. Turn on the Computer*xx* computer.

2. Log on to Computer*xx* as Administrator, using the password **Pa$$w0rd**.

   After the system starts up, it detects the newly installed network interface adapter card. If the adapter card you installed is identical to the one already in the computer, the system automatically installs and configures the appropriate driver.

3. If the newly installed network interface adapter card is different from the existing one, you might be prompted to supply a driver for the adapter. If this happens, follow the instructions in the Found New Hardware Wizard and either insert the driver disk supplied by your instructor or browse to the location of the driver.

4. Click Start, select Control Panel, right-click Network Connections, and then select Open.

   The Network Connections window appears.

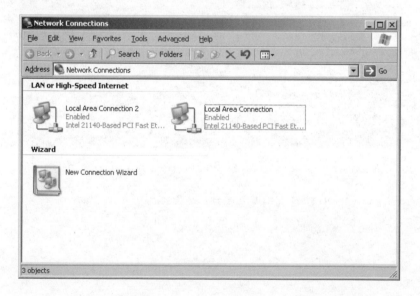

**QUESTION**   What icons appear in the Network Connections window?

5.  Click Start, select All Programs, select Accessories, and then select Command Prompt.

A Command Prompt window appears.

6.  In the Command Prompt window, type **ipconfig /all** and then press ENTER.

**QUESTION**   According to the Ipconfig display, what is the Internet Protocol (IP) address for Ethernet Adapter Local Area Connection?

**QUESTION**   What is the IP address for Ethernet Adapter Local Area Connection 2?

**QUESTION**   Based on these IP addresses, how can you tell which of the local area connections represents the newly installed network interface adapter card and which one represents the original network interface adapter card?

**NOTE**   Understanding Automatic Private IP Addressing (APIPA)
Computers running Windows that are configured to obtain IP addresses from a DHCP server automatically assign themselves a private IP address when they can't locate a DHCP server on the network. The APIPA addresses use the 169.254.0.0/16 network address, and the computers test them during the self-assignment process to prevent address duplication.

7. In the Network Connections window, select the icon representing the computer's original network interface adapter card, select Rename from the File menu, type **Classroom Network Connection** and then press ENTER.

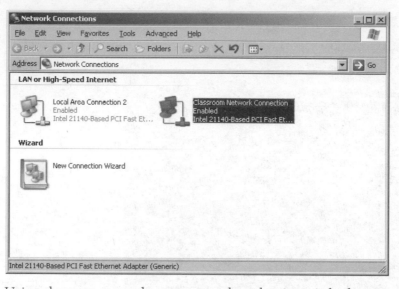

8. Using the same procedure, rename the other icon (which represents the newly installed network interface adapter card) **Lab Group Network Connection**

9. Close the Network Connections window.

10. Return to the Command Prompt window and type **ipconfig /all**.

> **QUESTION**   How does the Ipconfig display differ from when you ran it last?

11. Expand the Command Prompt window to show the entire Ipconfig display.

12. Take a screen shot (using ALT+PRNT SCRN) of the entire Command Prompt window containing the Ipconfig display, and then paste it into a WordPad document named LGxxLab03-1.rtf (where xx is the assigned number of your lab group).

    Your instructor will ask you to turn it in at the end of the lab.

13. Close the Command Prompt window.

14. Click Start, select Control Panel, and then select System.

    The System Properties dialog box appears.

**15.** Click the Hardware tab, and then click Device Manager.

The Device Manager window appears.

**16.** In the Device Manager window, expand the Network Adapters entry.

**17.** Select the first network interface adapter listed, and then from the Action menu, select Properties.

The Properties dialog box for the network interface adapter appears.

**18.** Click the Resources tab.

**QUESTION**  What hardware resources is the network interface adapter using?

**19.** Click OK to close the dialog box, and then open the Properties dialog box for the other network interface adapter in the system.

> **QUESTION**   What hardware resources is the second network interface adapter using?

**20.** Close all open dialog boxes.

# EXERCISE 3-3: CONFIGURING HARDWARE RESOURCES IN WINDOWS MANUALLY

**Estimated completion time: 20 minutes**

In this exercise you will manually install a hardware device and configure its resource settings. Then you will modify the settings for an existing hardware resource.

1. On Computerxx, click Start, select Control Panel, and then select Add Hardware.

   The Welcome To The Add Hardware Wizard page appears.

2. Click Next.

   The wizard searches for new plug and play (PnP) devices and then displays the Is The Hardware Connected? page.

3. Select Yes, I Have Already Connected The Hardware, and then click Next.

   A The Following Hardware Is Already Installed On Your Computer page appears.

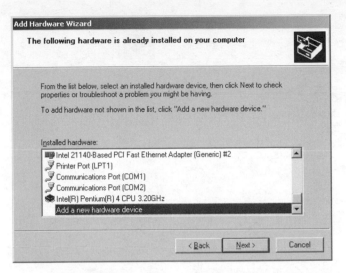

**4.** Scroll down to the bottom of the list, select Add A New Hardware Device, and then click Next.

A The Wizard Can Help You Install Other Hardware page appears.

**5.** Select Install The Hardware That I Manually Select From A List (Advanced), and then click Next.

The From The List Below, Select The Type Of Hardware You Are Installing page appears.

6. Scroll down, select Ports (COM & LPT), and then click Next.

   The Select The Device Driver You Want To Install For This Hardware page appears.

7. In the Model list, select Communications Port, and then click Next.

   A The Wizard Is Ready To Install Your Hardware page appears.

8. Click Next to install the hardware driver.

   The Completing The Add Hardware Wizard page appears.

9. Click Finish.

10. Open Device Manager, and then expand the Ports (COM & LPT) entry.

**QUESTION**   How is the newly installed Communications Port (COM3) different from the existing ones?

11.  Open the Properties dialog box for the COM3 port you just created, and then click the Resources tab.

**NOTE   Accessing Properties**   You can access Properties dialog boxes for most objects by right-clicking the object and selecting Properties from the context menu, as well as by using the Action menu.

**QUESTION**   What resources is the COM3 port using?

**12.** Click Set Configuration Manually.

The Resources tab assumes its usual appearance.

> **QUESTION**   What types of resource settings is a communications port configured to use?

> **QUESTION**   What resource settings are suggested in Basic Configuration 0000?

> **QUESTION**   Which of these settings are unacceptable? How can you tell?

**13.** Select the different configurations in the Setting Based On drop-down list to see if any of the preconfigured settings have no conflicts.

> **QUESTION**   What is the result?

**14.** Select Basic Configuration 0008 in the Settings Based On list.

15. Select IRQ from the Resource Settings list, and then click Change Setting.

The Edit Interrupt Request dialog box appears.

16. Scroll through the IRQ settings in the Value list.

> **QUESTION**   What IRQ settings can you use for this device that do not conflict with other devices?

17. Click Cancel twice to close the Edit Interrupt Request and Properties dialog boxes.

18. Close Device Manager, and then restart the computer.

19. Log on as Administrator, and then open Device Manager again.

   **QUESTION**    What is the status of the new Communications Port (COM3) device now?

20. Open the Properties dialog box for the Communications Port (COM3), click the Resources tab, and then click Set Configuration Manually.

   **QUESTION**    How is the Resources tab different from the way it was before you restarted the computer?

   **NOTE    Understanding Plug and Play (PnP)**    Each time a computer running Windows starts, the PnP hardware analysis process is repeated and the operating system assigns resources based on the hardware it has just detected in the computer. This is why the resource assignments change after the system restarts.

21. Select Basic Configuration 0001, and then change the interrupt request (IRQ) setting for the configuration.

   **QUESTION**    What IRQ settings are available now that do not conflict with other devices?

22. Select an IRQ setting that does not conflict.

23. Close the Properties dialog box by clicking OK.

24. Answer Yes when Device Manager prompts you to restart the system.

25. Log on, and then open Device Manager again.

26. Take a screen shot (using ALT+PRNT SCRN) of the Resources tab in the Communications Port (COM3) Properties dialog box, demonstrating that you have configured the device with no IRQ conflicts, and then paste it into a WordPad document named LGxxLab03- 2.rtf (where xx is the assigned number of your lab group).

   Your instructor will ask you to turn it in at the end of the lab.

> **QUESTION**   What is the status of the Communications Port (COM3) device now? Why?

# EXERCISE 3-4: BUILDING A LAN

**Estimated completion time: 10 minutes**

In this exercise you will assemble your lab group LAN by connecting your two computers to an Ethernet hub.

1. Close all applications on Computerxx, and then shut down the computer.

2. Make sure that the Computeryy system in your lab group is shut down as well.

3. Place the hub you examined in Exercise 2-4 of Lab 2 between your two computers.

4. Connect the hub's power cable to the hub and plug the other end into a power socket.

5. Using a CAT5 UTP cable, connect the network interface adapter in Computeryy to one of the standard ports on the hub.

6. Using another cable, connect the new network interface adapter you installed in Computerxx in Exercise 3-1 to another standard port on the hub.

   Make sure all the cable connectors are firmly seated in their jacks.

> **QUESTION**   What would happen if you connected one of the computers to the hub's uplink port? Why?

## EXERCISE 3-5: TESTING LAN COMMUNICATIONS

**Estimated completion time: 15 minutes**

In this exercise you will test the communications on your new lab group LAN.

1. Turn on Computer*xx*, and then check the light-emitting diodes (LEDs) on the lab group hub port and the network interface adapter.

   **QUESTION**  Are the LEDs at both ends of the connection lit?

2. Turn on Computer*yy* and check the LEDs on the hub port and the network interface adapter.

   **QUESTION**  Are the LEDs lit?

   **NOTE**  **Troubleshooting LAN Connections**  If the LEDs on both ends of the connection are not lit, check to see that the cables are seated correctly and that the hub and computer are both connected to a power supply. If this doesn't correct the problem, ask your instructor for help.

3. Log on to Computer*yy* as Administrator.

4. Run the **ipconfig /all** command on Computer*yy*, as you did on Computer*xx* in Exercise 3-2.

   **QUESTION**  What is Computer*yy*'s IP address?

5. Log on to Computer*xx* as Administrator.

6. On Computer*xx*, open a Command Prompt window, type **ping** plus Computer*yy*'s IP address (for example, **ping 169.254.224.25**), and then press ENTER.

**QUESTION**   What is the result of the Ping test, and what does this
indicate?

7. In the same Command Prompt window, type **ping 10.1.100.1** and
then press ENTER.

The address 10.1.100.1 is the IP address of the Server01 server on the
classroom network.

```
Command Prompt                                             _ | □ | x |

C:\Documents and Settings\Administrator>ping 10.1.100.1

Pinging 10.1.100.1 with 32 bytes of data:

Reply from 10.1.100.1: bytes=32 time=3ms TTL=128
Reply from 10.1.100.1: bytes=32 time=1ms TTL=128
Reply from 10.1.100.1: bytes=32 time=1ms TTL=128
Reply from 10.1.100.1: bytes=32 time=1ms TTL=128

Ping statistics for 10.1.100.1:
    Packets: Sent = 4, Received = 4, Lost = 0 (0% loss),
Approximate round trip times in milli-seconds:
    Minimum = 1ms, Maximum = 3ms, Average = 1ms

C:\Documents and Settings\Administrator>
```

**QUESTION**   What is the result of the test? What does this indicate?

8. On Computeryy, in the Command Prompt window, type **ping** plus the
IP address of Computerxx Lab Group Network Connection that you
noted in Exercise 3-2, and then press ENTER.

```
Command Prompt                                             _ | □ | x |

C:\Documents and Settings\Administrator>ping 169.254.104.70

Pinging 169.254.104.70 with 32 bytes of data:

Reply from 169.254.104.70: bytes=32 time=0ms TTL=128
Reply from 169.254.104.70: bytes=32 time=1ms TTL=128
Reply from 169.254.104.70: bytes=32 time<1ms TTL=128
Reply from 169.254.104.70: bytes=32 time<1ms TTL=128

Ping statistics for 169.254.104.70:
    Packets: Sent = 4, Received = 4, Lost = 0 (0% loss),
Approximate round trip times in milli-seconds:
    Minimum = 0ms, Maximum = 2ms, Average = 0ms

C:\Documents and Settings\Administrator>
```

**QUESTION**   What is the result of the Ping test?

9. On Computeryy, type **ping 10.1.100.1** and then press ENTER.

**QUESTION**    What is the result of this Ping test? What does this indicate?

# LAB REVIEW QUESTIONS

**Estimated completion time: 20 minutes**

1.  If you install a network interface adapter that is not PnP, what additional steps do you have to perform to complete the installation?

2.  In Exercise 3-2, why are the controls on the Resources tab that are used to manually configure the network interface adapter unavailable?

3.  What would happen if you connected Computeryy directly to Computerxx using a crossover cable and bypassing the hub? Explain your answer.

4.  What would happen if you connected one of your lab group computers to the hub's uplink port using a crossover cable? Explain your answer.

5.  What is the drawback of using a crossover cable connection instead of a hub?

6.  Why can Computerxx communicate with the classroom network, while Computeryy can't?

7.  What must you do to enable Computeryy to communicate with the Server01 server?

# LAB CHALLENGE 3-1: CONFIGURING HARDWARE RESOURCES IN LINUX

**Estimated completion time: 30 minutes**

In this challenge you will repeat some of the same tasks you performed in the exercises earlier in this lab, except you will perform them on a computer running a Linux operating system.

1. On the LinuxServer01 computer, log on as root, using the password supplied by your instructor.

> **NOTE** **Using the Root Account** The root account in Linux (and UNIX) has full privileges to all elements of the operating system, just like the Administrator account on a computer running Windows.

2. Click the Main Menu icon (represented by a red fedora hat), select System Settings, and then click Network.

   The Network Configuration dialog box appears.

3. Take a screen shot (using ALT+PRNT SCRN) of the Network Configuration dialog box and save it to a file called LGxxLab03-3.png (where xx is the assigned number of your lab group).

   Your instructor will review this screen shot at the end of the lab.

4. Using only the controls in the Network Configuration dialog box, discover the information needed to complete as much of the following table as possible:

| Parameter | Value |
| --- | --- |
| Nickname | |
| MAC address | |
| IP address | |
| Subnet mask | |
| Default gateway address | |
| Primary DNS server | |
| Interrupt (IRQ) | |
| Base (I/O) address | |

> **QUESTION** Which of the table cells were you unable to fill?

5. Using the Network Configuration dialog box, list the steps needed to manually configure the IRQ and I/O Address settings, but do not actually change the settings.

6. Open a terminal window by clicking the Main Menu icon, selecting System Tools, and choosing Terminal. Then use the Ifconfig command to display configuration information for the network interface adapter.

7. Type **ifconfig > LGxxLab03.txt** in the Terminal window, where *xx* is the number assigned to your lab group, to redirect the output of the Ifconfig program to a text file. Leave the file in place on the computer, where your instructor can review it.

8. Complete the remaining cells in the table.

9. Deactivate the eth0 device and take a screen shot (using ALT+PRNT SCRN) showing the device as deactivated, and then save the screen shot to a file called LGxxLab03-4.png (where *xx* is the assigned number of your lab group).

   Your instructor will review this screen shot at the end of the lab.

10. Reactivate the eth0 device.

11. Log off the system.

# LAB 4
# ANALYZING ETHERNET TRAFFIC

**This lab contains the following exercises and activities:**

- Exercise 4-1: Installing Active Directory

- Exercise 4-2: Joining a Domain

- Exercise 4-3: Capturing Ethernet Traffic

- Exercise 4-4: Analyzing Ethernet Addresses

- Exercise 4-5: Analyzing Ethernet Frame Types

- Lab Review Questions

- Lab Challenge 4-1: Analyzing Ethertypes

## BEFORE YOU BEGIN

To complete this lab, you will need to get the following materials from your instructor:

- The two-digit number assigned to your lab group. This number forms the name of your group (LG*xx*, where *xx* is the number assigned to your group).

- Access to a computer with an Internet connection or, alternatively, access to a recent organizationally unique identifier (OUI) table, supplied by your instructor.

**After completing this lab, you will be able to:**

- Install Active Directory directory service on a computer running Microsoft Windows Server 2003.

- Join a computer to a Windows Server 2003 domain.

- Capture and analyze Ethernet traffic.

**Estimated lesson time: 125 minutes**

## SCENARIO

You are the new network administrator for Contoso, Ltd., a small company that runs a network with multiple servers running Windows Server 2003 and workstations running Microsoft Windows XP and Microsoft Windows 2000. You are in the process of examining the traffic on the network, using the Network Monitor application included with Windows Server 2003. Because you have trained on a Token Ring network, this is your first experience with Ethernet, so you want to examine the Ethernet headers in the frames captured from the network. First, however, you must promote one of your computers running Windows Server 2003 to a domain controller and create a new domain, and then you must join workstations to that domain.

## EXERCISE 4-1: INSTALLING ACTIVE DIRECTORY

**Estimated completion time: 20 minutes**

In this exercise you will install Active Directory on Computerxx and create a new domain for your lab group.

1. Log on to Computerxx as Administrator, using the password **Pa$$w0rd**.

2. Click Start, and then select Run.

   The Run dialog box appears.

3. In the Open text box, type **dcpromo** and then click OK.

   The Active Directory Installation Wizard launches.

4. Click Next to bypass the Welcome page.

   The Operating System Compatibility page appears.

5. Click Next.

   The Domain Controller Type page appears.

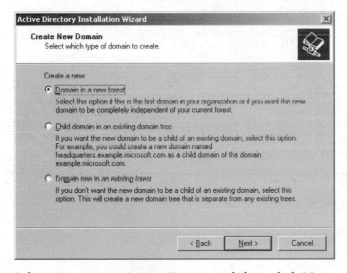

**6.** Click Next to use the default Domain Controller For A New Domain option.

The Create New Domain page appears.

**7.** Select Domain In A New Forest, and then click Next.

The New Domain Name page appears.

8. In the Full DNS Name For New Domain text box, type **lg*xx*.contoso.com** (where *xx* is the number assigned to your lab group), and then click Next.

   The NetBIOS Domain Name page appears.

9. Click Next to accept the default NetBIOS name for the new domain.

   The Database And Log Folders page appears.

10. Click Next to accept the default database and log folder values, and then click Next again.

    The Shared System Volume page appears.

11. Click Next to accept the default Shared System Volume location, and then click Next again.

    The DNS Registration Diagnostics page appears.

**12.** Select Install And Configure The DNS Server On This Computer, and then click Next.

The Permissions page appears.

**13.** Click Next to accept the default Permissions Compatible Only With Windows 2000 Or Windows Server 2003 Operating Systems option, and then click Next.

The Directory Services Restore Mode Administrator Password page appears.

**14.** In the Password and Confirm Password text boxes, type **Pa$$w0rd** and then click Next.

The Summary page appears.

**15.** Review the information presented on the Summary page, and then click Next.

The wizard proceeds to install Active Directory and create the new domain.

> **NOTE   Please Wait**   This procedure might take several minutes, and you might be prompted to insert the Windows Server 2003 installation CD-ROM. If this prompt occurs, click OK and browse to the \Win2k3\i386 folder on the computer's C drive.

**16.** During the Active Directory installation process, take a screen shot (using ALT+PRNT SCRN) of the active window, and then paste it into a WordPad document named LGxxLab04-1.rtf (where xx is the assigned number of your lab group).

Your instructor will ask you to turn it in at the end of the lab.

If you see an Optional Networking Components message box stating that your computer is using a dynamically assigned Internet Protocol (IP) address, click OK to ignore this warning.

17. On the Completing The Active Directory Installation Wizard page, click Finish.

An Active Directory Installation Wizard message box appears, informing you that you must restart the computer.

18. Click Restart Now.

19. When the computer has restarted, log on again as Administrator.

20. Open a Command Prompt window and execute the **ipconfig /all** command.

> **QUESTION**   What is the IP address of the Lab Group Network Connection interface on Computerxx?

## EXERCISE 4-2: JOINING A DOMAIN

**Estimated completion time: 15 minutes**

In this exercise you will join Computeryy to the domain you created on Computerxx.

1. Log on to Computeryy as Administrator.

2. Click Start, select Control Panel, select Network Connections, right-click Local Area Connection, and then select Properties.

The Local Area Connection Properties dialog box appears.

3. Select the Internet Protocol (TCP/IP) component, and then click Properties.

The Internet Protocol (TCP/IP) Properties dialog box appears.

**4.** Select Use The Following DNS Server Addresses.

**5.** Type the IP address of Computer*xx*'s Lab Group Network Connection interface in the Preferred DNS Server text box, and then click OK.

**6.** Click Close to close the Local Area Connection Properties dialog box.

> **QUESTION**   Why do you need to configure Computer*yy* to use Computer*xx* as its Domain Name System (DNS) server?

**7.** Click Start, select Control Panel, and then select System.

The System Properties dialog box appears.

**8.** Click the Computer Name tab, and then click Change.

The Computer Name Changes dialog box appears.

**9.** Select the Domain option, type **lgxx** in the text box (where *xx* is the number assigned to your lab group), and then click OK.

Another Computer Name Changes dialog box appears, prompting you for the name and password of an account with permission to join the domain.

**10.** Type **Administrator** in the User Name text box and **Pa$$w0rd** in the Password text box, and then click OK.

A Computer Name Changes message box appears, welcoming you to the lg*xx* domain.

**11.** Take a screen shot (using ALT+PRNT SCRN) of the Computer Name Changes message box, and then paste it into a WordPad document named LGxxLab04-2.rtf.

Your instructor will ask you to turn it in at the end of the lab.

**12.** Click OK.

A Computer Name Changes message box appears, informing you to restart the computer.

**13.** Click OK.

**14.** Click OK to close the System Properties dialog box.

A System Settings Change message box appears, asking if you want to restart the computer now.

**15.** Click Yes.

The computer restarts.

**16.** When the computer has restarted, log on to the LG*xx* domain as Administrator, using the password **Pa$$w0rd**.

**QUESTION**   If Computer*xx* was configured to use the password Pa$$w0rd01 and Computer*yy* was configured to use the password Pa$$w0rd02, which password would you have to use to log on to the LG*xx* domain?

# EXERCISE 4-3: CAPTURING ETHERNET TRAFFIC

**Estimated completion time: 15 minutes**

In this exercise you will use Network Monitor to capture a sample of your lab group network's Ethernet traffic.

1. On Computer*xx*, start Network Monitor. If you get a message that your default network is invalid, click OK.

2. Configure Network Monitor to capture traffic using the Lab Group Network Connection interface.

3. Load the address file named Addresses.adr you created and saved in Lab 1.

> **MORE INFO**   **Configuring Network Monitor**   To review the Network Monitor configuration process, refer to Lab 1.

4. Click the Start Capture button on the toolbar to begin capturing data.

5. On Computer*yy*, open a Command Prompt window. Then type **copy \\computer*xx*\windist\\*.* c:\win2k3\i386 /y** and press ENTER.

   The system copies files from Computer*xx* to Computer*yy*, overwriting the existing copies.

6. Wait about 5 minutes, and then click the Stop Capture button in Network Monitor on Computer*xx*.

7. On Computer*yy*, press CTRL+C to cancel the copy process and then run the **ipconfig /all** command in the Command Prompt window.

> **QUESTION**   What is the hardware address of Computer*yy*'s Local Area Connection interface?

8. In Network Monitor on Computer*xx*, locate an entry containing Computer*yy*'s hardware address in the Lab Group Network Connection

Capture window and create a permanent name mapping of that address to the name Computeryy, as you did for Computerxx in Lab 1.

> **QUESTION**   How many frames did Computeryy receive from Computerxx?

9.  Select the element in the Lab Group Network Connection Capture window that displays the number of frames Computeryy received from Computerxx, take a screen shot (using ALT+PRNT SCRN) of the entire Microsoft Network Monitor window, and then paste the screen shot into a WordPad document named LGxxLab04-3.rtf.

    Your instructor will ask you to turn it in at the end of the lab.

10. Leave Network Monitor open for the next exercise.

## EXERCISE 4-4: ANALYZING ETHERNET ADDRESSES

### Estimated completion time: 15 minutes

In this exercise you will examine the Ethernet addresses in the traffic sample you captured in Exercise 4-3.

1.  In Network Monitor on Computerxx, click the Display Captured Data button on the toolbar.

    The Capture: # Summary window appears.

2. Scroll down in the list and select a frame that contains the values shown in the following table:

| Src MAC Addr | Dst MAC Addr | Protocol | Description |
| --- | --- | --- | --- |
| Computerxx | Computeryy | NBT | SS Session Message Cont., 1460 bytes |

3. Double-click the frame to display the Detail and Hex panes.

4. In the Detail pane, expand the Frame heading.

**QUESTION**   What is the total size of the frame?

5. Expand the Ethernet heading.

**QUESTION**   What is the size of the frame's Ethernet header?

**QUESTION**   What is the value of the Destination Address field in the Ethernet header?

**QUESTION**   What is the OUI for the frame's destination address?

**QUESTION**   What is the significance of the OUI?

6. Using the search engine provided by the Institute of Electrical and Electronics Engineers (IEEE) at *http://standards.ieee.org/regauth/oui/index.shtml* or the list provided by your instructor, look up the OUI of the destination address.

**QUESTION**   Who manufactured the network interface adapter in the destination system (Computeryy)?

**QUESTION**   Who manufactured the network interface adapter in the source system (Computerxx)?

7. Leave Network Monitor open for the next exercise.

## EXERCISE 4-5: ANALYZING ETHERNET FRAME TYPES

**Estimated completion time: 15 minutes**

In this exercise you will examine the formats used by the various frames in the traffic sample you captured.

1. In Network Monitor on Computerxx, examine the structure of the Ethernet header in the frame you selected in Exercise 4-4.

**QUESTION**   Which Ethernet frame format was used by the computer that generated the frame?

**QUESTION**   How can you tell?

**QUESTION**   What is the Ethertype value in the frame and what protocol does it represent?

2. Scroll down to the bottom of the Summary pane and select the frame with STATS in the Protocol column.

The STATS is not an actual network frame at all, but rather an implementation of a protocol called TRAIL, which Network Monitor uses to track statistics about the current traffic capture.

**QUESTION**   What is the value of the 2 bytes following the source address in the frame's Ethernet header?

**QUESTION**   Which Ethernet frame format is this frame using?

**QUESTION**   How can you tell?

3. Expand the LLC heading in the frame.

**QUESTION**   What is the value of the DSAP and SSAP fields in the LLC header?

**QUESTION**   What is the significance of this value?

**4.** Expand the SNAP header in the frame.

**QUESTION**   What is the function of the Etype value in the SNAP header?

**5.** Click the Toggle Summary Pane and Toggle Hex Pane buttons in the toolbar so that the Detail pane fills the Network Monitor window.

**6.** Take a screen shot (using ALT+PRNT SCRN) of the Network Monitor window, showing the expanded Ethernet, LLC, and SNAP headings, and then paste the screen shot into a WordPad document named LGxxLab04-4.rtf (where *xx* is the assigned number of your lab group).

Your instructor will ask you to turn it in at the end of the lab.

**7.** Close the Network Monitor window.

It's not necessary to save the capture, but make sure you save the changes you made to your address file as you close the application.

# LAB REVIEW QUESTIONS

**Estimated completion time: 15 minutes**

**1.** How does Network Monitor know that the field following the source address contains an Ethertype measurement, not a Length measurement?

**2.** How can you tell the size of the Ethernet header in Exercise 4-4 based only on the Network Monitor display?

**3.** What would an Ethernet network be unable to do if the frames did not have an Ethertype value or its LLC/SNAP equivalent?

4. What would be the result if, in Exercise 4-3, you failed to load the address file you created in Lab 1?

# LAB CHALLENGE 4-1: ANALYZING ETHERTYPES

**Estimated completion time: 30 minutes**

At this time, all of the traffic on your lab group network uses Transmission Control Protocol/ Internet Protocol (TCP/IP) and virtually all TCP/IP traffic is carried inside IP datagrams. Because IP is the chief network layer protocol, the vast majority of the Ethernet frames transmitted over the network contains the Ethertype value 0x0800. There is one exception, however: the Address Resolution Protocol (ARP) is a TCP/IP protocol that is not encapsulated in IP datagrams.

Your task for this challenge is to generate a sample of ARP traffic on your lab group network, capture the traffic using Network Monitor, and display the frames containing an Ethertype value other than 0x0800. As you complete the challenge, keep the following hints and requirements in mind:

- You must create a capture filter in Network Monitor that enables the application to capture only ARP traffic.

- You can generate ARP traffic by using the Ping utility with a computer name instead of an IP address, such as **ping computeryy**.

To complete this challenge, do the following:

1. Write out a procedure detailing each step of the process.

2. Take screen shots of the Capture Filter window, containing the completed ARP capture filter, and of the Capture: # Summary window, containing only ARP traffic and with the ARP Ethertype highlighted in the Ethernet header. Paste the screen shots into separate WordPad documents named LGxxLab04-5.rtf and LGxxLab04-6.rtf (where xx is the assigned number of your lab group). You will turn them in at the end of the lab.

3. Finally, save the traffic sample as a file called LGxxLab04-6.cap, to turn in at the end of the lab.

## LAB 5
# NETWORK LAYER PROTOCOLS

**This lab contains the following exercises and activities:**

■ Exercise 5-1: Converting Binaries to Decimals

■ Exercise 5-2: Calculating Subnet Masks

■ Exercise 5-3: Analyzing IP Traffic

■ Exercise 5-4: Installing IPX

■ Exercise 5-5: Capturing IPX Traffic

■ Exercise 5-6: Analyzing IPX Traffic

■ Lab Review Questions

## BEFORE YOU BEGIN

To complete this lab, you will need to get the following materials from your instructor:

■ The two-digit number assigned to your lab group. This number forms the name of the lab group (LG*xx*, where *xx* is the number assigned to your group).

■ A network address, unique to your lab group, assigned by your instructor.

**After completing this lab, you will be able to:**

■ Convert binary numbers to decimals.

■ Calculate the subnet mask to use on a Transmission Control Protocol/Internet Protocol (TCP/IP) network.

■ Install the Internetwork Packet Exchange (IPX) protocol on a computer running Microsoft Windows Server 2003 and control the protocol bindings.

■ Capture and analyze IPX traffic.

**Estimated lesson time: 135 minutes**

## SCENARIO

You are the new network administrator for Contoso, Ltd., a small company that runs a network with servers running Windows Server 2003 and workstations running Microsoft Windows XP and Microsoft Windows 2000. You are examining the traffic on the network, using the Network Monitor application included with Windows Server 2003. The company network uses TCP/IP for most of its communications, but there is also an old Novell NetWare server on the network that hosts a vital company database. Therefore, you need to become familiar with network traffic generated by IPX, as well Internet Protocol (IP) traffic.

## EXERCISE 5-1: CONVERTING BINARIES TO DECIMALS

**Estimated completion time: 15 minutes**

In this and future labs, you will be asked to work with IP address and subnet mask values in binary form and convert the binary values to the decimals normally used by network administrators. Although many calculators and software products can perform these conversions for you, the ability to convert binaries to decimals manually is a valuable skill that you might need one day.

> **NOTE**   **Reviewing the Conversion Process**   *See the section entitled "Converting Binaries and Decimals" in Chapter 5 of the textbook to review the binary/decimal conversion process.*

Convert the following binary IP addresses and subnet masks into decimals (without using a calculator):

1. 11111111 11111111 11111111 11000000

2. 11000000 10101000 01010111 01110010

3. 00001010 00000001 00001110 11111101

4. 11111111 11111111 11100000 00000000

5. 10101100 00010000 10000111 00001001

6. 11111111 11111110 00000000 00000000

7. 11111111 11111111 11111111 11110000

8. 11001110 01001001 01110110 01100011

9. 10011101 00111100 11001001 11001000

10. 11111111 11111111 11111100 00000000

# EXERCISE 5-2: CALCULATING SUBNET MASKS

**Estimated completion time: 15 minutes**

Up to now your lab group network has been using IP addresses assigned by the Windows Server 2003 operating system, using a system called Automatic Private Internet Protocol Addressing (APIPA). In this lab and the next two labs, you will calculate new IP addresses and other TCP/IP configuration parameters for your lab group and implement them on your computers.

In this exercise you will calculate the subnet mask that you will use to configure the computers in your lab group. Your instructor will give you a network address intended for your lab group network alone. Do not duplicate the addresses used by the other lab groups. You must perform all of your calculations manually; do not use Windows Calculator or any other calculating program or device.

> **IMPORTANT**   If you do not have an instructor to supply you with a network address, use 10.2.128.0/19.

1. Write down the network address given to you by your instructor.

    > **QUESTION**   What IP address class does your network address belong to?

    > **NOTE   IP Address Classes**   Consult Table 5-2 in Chapter 5 of the textbook if you're not sure what IP address class your network address belongs to.

    > **QUESTION**   What is the size of the network identifier in the class of address you have been assigned (in bits)?

2. Subtract the number of network identifier bits from the number following the slash in the address.

    > **QUESTION**   What is the result?

    > **QUESTION**   What does this value represent?

3. Calculate the value of $2^x - 2$, where $x$ is the value you calculated in step 2.

**QUESTION**  What is the result?

**QUESTION**  What does this value represent?

4. Subtract the number following the slash in the address from 32.

**QUESTION**  What is the result?

**QUESTION**  What does this value represent?

5. Calculate the value of $2^x - 2$, where $x$ is the value you calculated in step 4.

**QUESTION**  What is the result?

**QUESTION**  What does this value represent?

6. Write the number of ones corresponding to the value after the slash in the address.

   For example, if the address was 172.23.47.0/24, you would write 24 ones, as follows:

   111111111111111111111111

7. Next, add zeros after the ones to reach a total of 32 bits, as in the following example:

   11111111111111111111111100000000

8. Now split the 32-bit value into four groups of eight bits each and convert each of the 8-bit binary numbers to decimal form, as in the following example:

   11111111  11111111  11111111  00000000

   255         255         255         0

9. Write the four 8-bit decimal numbers, using dotted decimal notation, as in the following example:

   255.255.255.0

   This value is the subnet mask that you will use for your lab group network. In Lab 6 of this manual, you will calculate the IP addresses for your network, and in Lab 7 you will configure the computers to use them.

# EXERCISE 5-3: ANALYZING IP TRAFFIC

**Estimated completion time: 15 minutes**

In this exercise you will capture a traffic sample from your lab group network and analyze the contents of the IP header in the frames.

1. On Computer*xx*, log on as Administrator using the password **Pa$$w0rd**.

2. Launch Network Monitor and configure it to capture traffic from your Lab Group Network Connection interface.

   Do not forget to load the address file you created in Lab 1.

3. Start copying the contents of the Windist share on Computer*yy* to the C:\Win2k3\i386 folder on Computer*xx*, overwriting all existing files.

   > **MORE INFO** *Copying Windist Files* To review the process of copying the Windist files, refer to Exercise 4-3 in Lab 4.

4. Capture a sample of the traffic on your lab group network, using Network Monitor. After a couple of minutes, stop the capture and abort the copy process.

5. Display the captured data.

6. Double-click one of the frames in the Capture: # Summary window.

   The Detail and Hex panes appear, containing information about the selected frame.

7. Take a screen shot (using Alt+Prnt Scrn) of the Microsoft Network Monitor window. Then paste it into a WordPad document named LGxxLab05-1.rtf (where xx is the assigned number of your lab group).

Your instructor will ask you to turn it in at the end of the lab.

8. In the Detail pane, expand the IP heading, and then expand each of the subheadings below it.

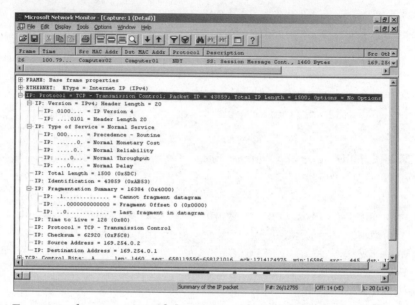

9. Examine the contents of the IP header and answer the following questions:

**QUESTION** What version of IP are the computers on the network using?

**QUESTION** Under what conditions could the value of the Version field be different?

**QUESTION** What is the length of the IP header in the frame you are studying?

**QUESTION** How much data (in bytes) is being carried in the datagram?

**QUESTION** How can you tell?

**QUESTION** Has the datagram you are studying been fragmented?

**QUESTION** How can you tell?

**QUESTION** Why has the datagram not been fragmented?

**QUESTION** What is the default Time-To-Live (TTL) value set by computers running Windows?

**QUESTION** What is the TTL value for the frame you are studying?

**QUESTION** Why are both values the same?

**QUESTION** What protocol is encapsulated within the IP datagram?

10. Leave Network Monitor open for use in later exercises.

# EXERCISE 5-4: INSTALLING IPX

**Estimated completion time: 15 minutes**

In this exercise you will install Microsoft's version of the IPX protocol suite so that you can later capture a sample of IPX traffic for analysis.

1. On Computerxx, click Start, select Control Panel, right-click Network Connections, and then select Open.

   The Network Connections window appears.

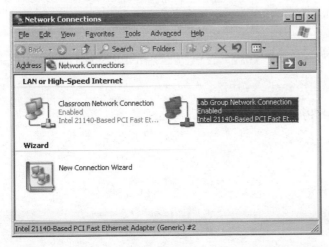

2. Right-click the Lab Group Network Connection icon, and then select Properties.

   The Lab Group Network Connection Properties dialog box appears.

**QUESTION**   What networking software components are currently associated with the Lab Group Network Connection interface?

**QUESTION**   Which of these components is not being used by the Lab Group Network Connection?

**QUESTION**   How can you tell?

3. Click Install.

The Select Network Component Type dialog box appears.

4. Select Protocol, and then click Add.

The Select Network Protocol dialog box appears.

5. Select NWLink IPX/SPX/NetBIOS Compatible Transport Protocol, and then click OK.

   The NWLink NetBIOS and NWLink IPX/SPX/NetBIOS Compatible Transport Protocol modules are added to the components list.

6. Take a screen shot (using Alt+Prnt Scrn) of the Lab Group Network Connection Properties dialog box and then paste it into a WordPad document named LGxxLab05_2.rtf (where xx is the assigned number of your lab group).

   Your instructor will ask you to turn it in at the end of the lab.

7. Click Close to close the Lab Group Network Connection Properties dialog box.

8. Open the Classroom Network Connection Properties dialog box.

> **QUESTION**   What networking software components are currently associated with the Classroom Network Connection interface?

9. On Computeryy, log on as Administrator of the LGxx domain.

10. On Computeryy, repeat steps 1–7 to install the NWLink IPX/SPX/Net-BIOS Compatible Transport Protocol module on Local Area Connection.

# EXERCISE 5-5: CAPTURING IPX TRAFFIC

**Estimated completion time: 15 minutes**

In this exercise you will capture a sample of IPX traffic from your lab group network.

1. On Computerxx, repeat steps 2–4 from Exercise 5-3, and capture a sample of traffic from your lab group network.

2. Examine the traffic sample in Network Monitor's Capture: # Summary window.

**QUESTION**   Which network layer protocol did the computers use to communicate during the capture?

**QUESTION**   How can you tell?

3. Switch to the Network Connections window on Computerxx and, from the Advanced menu, select Advanced Settings.

The Advanced Settings dialog box appears.

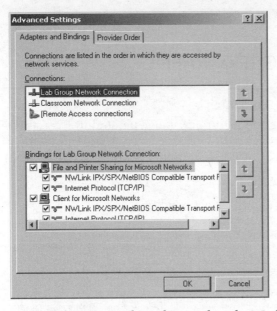

**4.** In the Adapters And Bindings tab, select Lab Group Network Connection from the Connections list.

**5.** In the Bindings For Lab Group Network Connection list, clear the two Internet Protocol (TCP/IP) check boxes for the File And Printer Sharing For Microsoft Networks and Client For Microsoft Networks modules, and then click OK.

**6.** Use Network Monitor to capture another traffic sample from the lab group network.

**QUESTION**   Which network protocols are the computers using to communicate now?

7. Leave Network Monitor open for the next exercise.

# EXERCISE 5-6: ANALYZING IPX TRAFFIC

**Estimated completion time: 15 minutes**

In this exercise you will examine the IPX traffic you generated in Exercise 5-5.

1. Double-click a frame in the Capture: # Summary window to display the Detail and Hex panes.

2. In the Detail pane, expand the Ethernet heading.

**QUESTION**   How is the Ethernet header in this IPX frame different from those in the IP packets you examined in Lab 4 in this manual?

3. Expand the IPX heading, as well as the Destination Address Summary and Source Address Summary subheadings, and then answer the following questions:

```
Microsoft Network Monitor - [Capture: 3 (Detail)]                        _ |8| X|
File  Edit  Display  Tools  Options  Window  Help                        _ |8| X|
[toolbar icons]
Frame | Time      | Src MAC Addr | Dst MAC Addr | Protocol | Description                              | Src Ot|
1     | 80.035085 | Computer01   | Computer02   | NBIPX    | Session Data, Ack, Recv Seq 0xAC46, 0xAC4B ... | 0.0003I
2     | 80.035085 | Computer01   | Computer02   | NBIPX    | Session Data, Ack, Recv Seq 0xAC48, 0xAC4D ... | 0.0003I
3     | 80.035085 | Computer01   | Computer02   | NBIPX    | Session Data, Ack, Recv Seq 0xAC4A, 0xAC4F ... | 0.0003I
4     | 80.035085 | Computer02   | Computer01   | NBIPX    | Session Data                             | 0.0003I
5     | 80.035085 | Computer02   | Computer01   | NBIPX    | Session Data                             | 0.0003I
6     | 80.035085 | Computer02   | Computer01   | NBIPX    | Session Data                             | 0.0003I

+ FRAME: Base frame properties
- ETHERNET: 802.3, DataLength = 52
  + ETHERNET: Destination address = 0003FF70B8B1
  + ETHERNET: Source address = 0003FF72B8B1
  - ETHERNET: Data Length : 0x0034 (52)
- LLC: Unnumbered (U) Frame, Command Frame, DSAP = Novell IPX/SPX, SSAP = Novell IPX/SPX
- IPX: NetBIOS Packet - 0.0003FF72B8B1.455 -> 0.0003FF70B8B1.455 - 0 Hops
    - IPX: Checksum = 65535 (0xFFFF)
    - IPX: IDP Length = 48 (0x30)
    - IPX: Transport control = 0 (0x0)
    - IPX: Packet type = IPX
    - IPX: Destination Address Summary 0.0003FF70B8B1.455
      -- IPX: Destination IPX Address = 00000000.0003FF70B8B1
      -- IPX: Destination Net Number = 0 (0x0)
      -- IPX: Destination Socket Number = NetBIOS
    - IPX: Source Address Summary 0.0003FF72B8B1.455
      -- IPX: Source IPX Address = 00000000.0003FF72B8B1
      -- IPX: Source Net Number = 0 (0x0)
      -- IPX: Source Socket Number = NetBIOS
    - IPX: Data: Number of data bytes remaining = 18 (0x0012)
+ NBIPX: Session Data, Ack, Recv Seq 0xAC46, 0xAC4B Bytes Received

Internet Packet Exchange Protocol (I F#: 1/12624      Off: 17 (x11)    L: 4 (x4)
```

**QUESTION**   Is there a network layer error detection mechanism in the frame, and if so, what field implements it?

**QUESTION**   How much data is being carried in the IPX datagram?

**QUESTION**   How can you tell?

**QUESTION**   What is the value of the Transport Control field?

**QUESTION**   What is the value given in the Destination Address Summary entry?

**QUESTION**   What is the significance of this value?

4. Take a screen shot (using Alt+Prnt Scrn) of the Windows Network Monitor window, and then paste it into a WordPad document named LGxxLab05-3.rtf (where xx is the assigned number of your lab group).

   Your instructor will ask you to turn it in at the end of the lab.

5. In the Network Connections window, open the Advanced Settings dialog box again.

6. Select the two Internet Protocol (TCP/IP) check boxes you cleared in Exercise 5-5, clear the two NWLink IPX/SPX/NetBIOS Compatible Transport Protocol check boxes, and then click OK.

## LAB REVIEW QUESTIONS

**Estimated completion time: 15 minutes**

1. What would be the most obvious difference in the IP header of a captured frame if the value of the Version field was different?

2. How does the Ethernet protocol indicate when IPX generated a frame's payload?

3. What does a value greater than 20 in an IP header's Length field indicate?

4. Why is the value of the Transport Control field in your captured IPX frames zero?

5. What effect, if any, does increasing the size of the subnet identifier in a subnet mask have on the number of subnets you can create on the network?

6. What effect, if any, does increasing the size of the subnet identifier in a subnet mask have on the number of hosts you can create on the network?

7. What effect, if any, does increasing the size of the subnet identifier in a subnet mask have on the class of the address?

## LAB 6
# TRANSPORT LAYER PROTOCOLS

**This lab contains the following exercises and activities:**

■ Exercise 6-1: Converting Decimals to Binaries

■ Exercise 6-2: Calculating IP Addresses

■ Exercise 6-3: Capturing UDP Traffic

■ Exercise 6-4: Analyzing UDP Traffic

■ Exercise 6-5: Capturing TCP Traffic

■ Exercise 6-6: Analyzing TCP Traffic

■ Lab Review Questions

■ Lab Challenge 6-1: Calculating Additional Subnets

■ Lab Challenge 6-2: Advanced Display Filtering

## BEFORE YOU BEGIN

To complete this lab, you will need to get the following materials from your instructor:

■ The two-digit number assigned to your lab group. This number forms the name of your group (LG*xx*, where *xx* is the number assigned to your group).

■ The network address, unique to your lab group, assigned by your instructor for Lab 5 in this manual.

**After completing this lab, you will be able to:**

■ Convert decimal numbers to binaries.

■ Calculate the Internet Protocol (IP) addresses to use on a Transmission Control Protocol/Internet Protocol (TCP/IP) network.

■ Capture and analyze User Datagram Protocol (UDP) and Transmission Control Protocol (TCP) traffic.

**Estimated lesson time:   135 minutes**

## SCENARIO

You are the new network administrator for Contoso, Ltd., a small company that runs a network with multiple servers running Microsoft Windows Server 2003 and workstations running Microsoft Windows XP and Microsoft Windows 2000. You are examining the traffic on the network, using the Network Monitor application included with Windows Server 2003. To fully understand the nature of the traffic on the network, you are comparing the messages generated by the UDP and TCP protocols and examining their functions.

## EXERCISE 6-1: CONVERTING DECIMALS TO BINARIES

**Estimated completion time: 15 minutes**

In Exercise 5-1 in Lab 5 of this manual, you converted binary numbers to decimals. Being able to make this conversion enables you to calculate the IP addresses and subnet masks for a subnetted network. Converting decimals to binaries is also a valuable skill, which you will need in Exercise 6-2.

For each of the following addresses, specify the binary form of the network address and the subnet mask. Do not use a calculator or any software to perform the calculations.

> **NOTE**   Reviewing the Conversion Process   See the section titled "Converting Binaries and Decimals" in Chapter 5 of the textbook to review the binary/decimal conversion process.

1. 10.184.96.0/19

2. 192.168.3.16/29

3. 207.73.118.128/26

4. 172.16.28.0/22

5. 157.60.112.0/20

# EXERCISE 6-2: CALCULATING IP ADDRESSES

**Estimated completion time: 15 minutes**

In this exercise you will calculate the new IP addresses you will use on your lab group network, using the same network address that you used to calculate the subnet mask in Exercise 5-2 in Lab 5 of this manual. Perform all your calculations manually.

1. Create a paper worksheet, to be submitted to your instructor at the end of the lab, containing sufficient space for your calculations and a copy of Table 6-1.

**Table 6-1  Lab Group TCP/IP Configuration Parameters**

| | |
|---|---|
| Subnet mask | |
| Computerxx IP address | |
| Computeryy IP address | |
| Third IP address | |
| Last IP address | |

2. Copy the subnet mask value you created in Exercise 5-2 to the "Subnet mask" cell in Table 6-1.

3. Using the network address supplied by your instructor, create an IP address diagram on your worksheet, consisting of 32 letters, with letter N's representing network identifier bits, letter S's representing subnet identifier bits, and letter H's representing host identifier bits. For example, if the supplied network address were 172.23.47.0/26, you would write the following:

   NNNNNNNN NNNNNNNN SSSSSSSS SSHHHHHH

4. Convert the four decimal numbers before the slash in the network address into binary form and write them on your worksheet below the IP address diagram, as in the following example:

   NNNNNNNN NNNNNNNN SSSSSSSS SSHHHHHH
   10101100 00010111 00101111 00000000

5. Compare the binary version of the network address you just calculated to the diagram you created in step 1 and copy the network identifier and subnet identifier bits only, as in the following example:

   NNNNNNNN NNNNNNNN SSSSSSSS SSHHHHHH
   10101100 00010111 00101111 00

6. To calculate the first IP address in the subnet your instructor has assigned you, add binary host identifier bits with a total decimal value of 1 to the address you wrote in step 5, and write down the resulting 32-bit binary value on your worksheet.

   For any binary number consisting of x bits, a decimal value of 1 would be $(x - 1)$ zeros followed by a single 1. For example, a 6-bit binary number with a decimal value of 1 would be 000001, as in the following example:

   `10101100 00010111 00101111 00000001`

7. Convert the four 8-bit binary numbers you wrote down in step 6 into decimals and write them down on your worksheet, using dotted decimal notation, as in the following example:

   `172.23.47.1`

   This is the IP address value you will use for Computerxx. Write the address in the "Computerxx IP address" cell of Table 6-1.

8. To calculate the second IP address in your assigned subnet, which you will use for Computeryy, repeat step 6, this time adding binary host identifier bits with a total decimal value of 2 to the address you wrote in step 5.

   The decimal number 2 in binary form is 10, so a 6-bit binary number with a decimal value of 2 would be 000010, as in the following example:

   `10101100 00010111 00101111 00000010`

9. Convert the four 8-bit binary numbers you wrote down in step 8 into decimals and write them on your worksheet, using dotted decimal notation, as in the following example:

   `172.23.47.2`

   This is the IP address value you will use for Computeryy. Write the address in the "Computeryy IP address" cell of Table 6-1.

10. In Lab 8, you will use the remaining addresses in your assigned subnet to create a scope on a Dynamic Host Configuration Protocol (DHCP) server. A scope is a range of IP addresses that the DHCP server can allocate to clients as needed. To determine the addresses to use for the scope, you must calculate the third and last IP addresses in your subnet. To calculate the third IP address, repeat step 6, adding a decimal value of 3 to the host identifier.

11. Convert the resulting binary value into decimals and write the dotted-decimal IP address in the "Third IP address" cell of Table 6-1.

12. To calculate the last IP address in the subnet, repeat step 6, but this time use the highest allowable value for the host identifier.

   For any binary host identifier consisting of x bits, the highest allowable value is (x − 1) ones followed by a single 0. For example, the highest allowable 6-bit host identifier would be 111110, as in the following example:

   `10101100 00010111 00101111 00111110`

   > **QUESTION**   Why can't you use a value of all ones for the last host in the subnet?

13. Convert the resulting binary value into decimals and write the dotted-decimal address in the "Last IP address" cell in Table 6-1.

14. Keep a copy of the completed table for yourself because you will need to refer to it in upcoming labs.

## EXERCISE 6-3: CAPTURING UDP TRAFFIC

**Estimated completion time: 15 minutes**
In this exercise you will generate network traffic that uses the UDP protocol and capture a sample of it by using Network Monitor.

1. On Computer*xx*, log on as Administrator, using the password **Pa$$w0rd**.

2. Launch Network Monitor and configure it to capture traffic from the Lab Group Network Connection interface.

   > **NOTE   Loading the Address Database**   Do not forget to load the address database file you created in Lab 1 of this manual.

3. Click Start Capture to begin capturing traffic.

4. On Computer*yy*, log on to the LG*xx* domain (where *xx* is the number assigned to your lab group), using the Administrator account.

5. Open a Command Prompt window and type **nslookup computer*xx* computer*xx***, and then press ENTER.

Nslookup is a utility that enables you to send Domain Name System (DNS) queries to specific servers on the network. In the command line you are using, the first Computerxx parameter specifies the host whose name you want to look up, and the second Computerxx parameter identifies the DNS server that you want to use to look up the host. In this particular instance, the host and the DNS server are the same computer.

**QUESTION**    What is the result of the Nslookup command?

**NOTE    Understanding Nslookup Output**    Nslookup also displays an error message stating that it can't find a server name for the IP address of the DNS server. This is normal because there are no reverse lookup records in the DNS database at this time.

**6.** When the Nslookup program finishes displaying its response, type **exit** in the Command Prompt window, and then press ENTER.

**7.** Return to Network Monitor on Computerxx and select Stop And View from the Capture menu.

Create a display filter in Network Monitor that will enable the display of frames containing only the DNS protocol.

8. Take a screen shot (using ALT+PRNT SCRN) of the Microsoft Network Monitor window with the display filter applied, and then paste it into a WordPad document named LGxxLab06-1.rtf (where *xx* is the assigned number of your lab group).

   Your instructor will ask you to turn it in at the end of the lab.

9. Leave Network Monitor open for the next exercise.

## EXERCISE 6-4: ANALYZING UDP TRAFFIC

**Estimated completion time: 15 minutes**

1. In Network Monitor on Computer*xx*, double-click the first DNS protocol frame appearing in the Capture: # Summary window.

   The Detail and Hex panes appear.

2. In the Detail pane, expand the UDP entry to display the contents of the UDP header. Then answer the following questions.

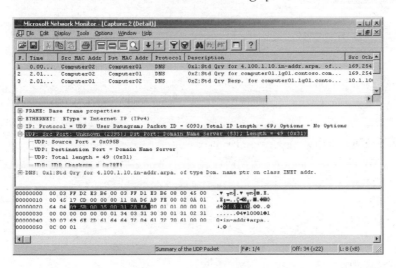

**QUESTION**   Based on the information in the Summary pane, which computer generated the frame you are examining?

**QUESTION**   Which computer received the frame?

**QUESTION**   What is the value of the frame's Destination Port?

**QUESTION**   What does this value mean?

**QUESTION**    What is the value of the message's Source Port field?

**QUESTION**    What does this value represent?

3. Scroll down in the summary window to the next DNS message on which Computeryy is the destination system.

**QUESTION**    Without looking at the Network Monitor screen, what should the Source Port value be for this message?

**QUESTION**    How can you tell?

**QUESTION**    What is the value of the Destination Port field?

**QUESTION**    Where did this value come from?

4. Close the Capture: # Summary window.

5. Leave Network Monitor open for the next exercise.

# EXERCISE 6-5: CAPTURING TCP TRAFFIC

**Estimated completion time: 10 minutes**

In this exercise you will generate TCP traffic on your network by connecting to the FTP server on Server01 and then capture a traffic sample by using Network Monitor.

1. In Network Monitor on Computer*xx*, configure the program to capture traffic from the Classroom Network Connection interface.

2. Click Start Capture. When you're prompted to save the existing capture session, click No.

3. On Computer*xx*, open a Command Prompt window, type **ftp server01** at the prompt, and then press ENTER.

> **QUESTION**   What happens?

4. Type **anonymous** and then press ENTER.

> **QUESTION**   What happens?

5. Type your full name, and then press ENTER.

> **QUESTION**   What happens?

6. Type **get eula.txt** and then press ENTER.

> **QUESTION**   What happens?

7. Type **quit** and press ENTER.

8. Close the Command Prompt window.

9. Switch to the Network Monitor window and click Stop And View Capture.

   The Capture: # Summary page appears.

10. Leave Network Monitor open for the next exercise.

# EXERCISE 6-6: ANALYZING TCP TRAFFIC

**Estimated completion time: 20 minutes**

In this exercise you will apply a display filter to the network traffic sample you just captured and examine the contents of the TCP headers.

1. In Network Monitor on Computerxx, create a display filter that enables the display of frames containing the TCP protocol only.

2. Take a screen shot (using ALT+PRNT SCRN) of the Microsoft Network Monitor window with the display filter applied, and then paste it into a WordPad document named LGxxLab06-2.rtf (where xx is the assigned number of your lab group).

Your instructor will ask you to turn it in at the end of the lab.

3. In the capture summary, locate a frame that contains SYN as its only control bit and double-click it to display the Detail and Hex panes.

   The value in the Description column for each TCP frame begins with a summary of the control bits in that frame, using their first initials.

4. Expand the TCP entry in the details pane to display the message header information. Then answer the following questions.

```
Microsoft Network Monitor - [Capture: 4 (Detail)]                                    _ □ ×
File  Edit  Display  Tools  Options  Window  Help                                    _ ₈ ×

F. Time     Src MAC Addr  Dst MAC Addr  Protocol  Description                         Src Oth
5  5.00...  Computer01    Server01      TCP       Control Bits: ....S., len:   0, seq: 69327...  10.1.10
6  5.00...  Server01      Computer01    TCP       Control Bits: .A..S., len:   0, seq: 383104...  SERVER0.
7  5.00...  Computer01    Server01      TCP       Control Bits: .A...., len:   0, seq: 69327...  10.1.10

⊞ FRAME: Base frame properties
⊞ ETHERNET:  EType = Internet IP (IPv4)
⊞ IP: Protocol = TCP - Transmission Control; Packet ID = 36532; Total IP Length = 48; Options = No Options
⊟ TCP: Control Bits: ....S., len:    0, seq: 693273745-693273746, ack:     0, win:16384, src: 4296  dst:
    TCP: Source Port = 0x10C8
    TCP: Destination Port = File Transfer [Control]
    TCP: Sequence Number = 693273745 (0x29528491)
    TCP: Acknowledgement Number = 0 (0x0)
  ⊞ TCP: Data Offset = 28 bytes
  ⊞ TCP: Flags = 0x02 : ....S.
    TCP: Window = 16384 (0x4000)
    TCP: Checksum = 0xA857
    TCP: Urgent Pointer = 0 (0x0)
  ⊟ TCP: Options
    ⊟ TCP: Maximum Segment Size Option
        TCP: Option Type = Maximum Segment Size
        TCP: Option Length = 4 (0x4)
        TCP: Maximum Segment Size = 1460 (0x5B4)
      TCP: Option Nop = 1 (0x1)
      TCP: Option Nop = 1 (0x1)
    ⊞ TCP: SACK Permitted Option

                          TCP protocol summary    F#: 5/69    Off: 34 (x22)   L: 28 (x1C)
```

**QUESTION**   What is the function of this frame?

**QUESTION**   Which computer initiated the handshake?

**QUESTION**   Which of the instructions you executed in the Command Prompt window in Exercise 6-5 initiated the handshake?

**QUESTION**   What is the Destination Port value in this frame, in decimal form?

**QUESTION**   How can you tell?

**QUESTION**   What is the maximum segment size specified by Computerxx?

**QUESTION**   How can you tell?

**QUESTION**   What is Computerxx's initial sequence number (ISN) value for this connection?

**QUESTION**   How do you know?

**QUESTION**   What is Computerxx's Acknowledgment Number value in this frame?

**QUESTION**   Why is the Acknowledgment Number value what it is?

**QUESTION**   Without looking at the Network Monitor screen, what is the Acknowledgment Number value going to be in Server01's SYN/ACK message?

**QUESTION**   How can you tell without looking?

**QUESTION**   What is the ISN supplied to Computerxx by Server01?

**QUESTION**   Based on this information and without looking at the Network Monitor screen, what will the Sequence Number and Acknowledgment Number values be for the Computerxx's ACK message that concludes the handshake?

**QUESTION**   How can you predict these values?

5. Scroll down the capture summary list and locate the frames that have "RETR eula.txt" and "150 Opening ASCII mode connection" in the Description column.

   RETR is the File Transfer Protocol (FTP) command that a client uses to retrieve a file from the server. The Opening ASCII Mode Connection message contains the FTP server's acknowledgment of the RETR command and signals the beginning of the file transfer.

6. Immediately following these two frames is another TCP handshake sequence. Examine the TCP headers in this handshake sequence and answer the following questions.

**NOTE**   **Analyzing TCP Handshake Messages**   Network Monitor provides timing information accurate to one millionth of a second, as demonstrated by the six decimal places displayed in the Time column. However, on a small local area network (LAN), it's possible for frames to appear out of sequence because the TCP message exchanges occur so quickly. If the three messages in your captured handshake sequences do not appear in the correct order (SYN, ACK/SYN, ACK), look at their respective Time values. You will probably see that two or all three of the messages have identical time stamps, which is why Network Monitor is displaying them in the wrong order.

**QUESTION**   What is the Source Port value for the SYN message initiating the handshake sequence?

**QUESTION**   Why is this port value different from the one used in the previous handshake?

7.  Scroll down in the capture summary and note the series of Data Transfer To Client messages sent by Server01, and then select the last of the Data Transfer To Client frames and examine its contents.

The Data Transfer To Client messages are the frames that contain the Eula.txt file that Server01 is sending to Computerxx.

**QUESTION**   How many messages does it take for Server01 to transmit the entire Eula.txt file?

QUESTION    What is the function of the frames transmitted from Computerxx to Server01 that are interspersed between the Data Transfer To Client messages?

QUESTION    In addition to delivering the last segment of the Eula.txt file, what other critical function does this frame perform?

QUESTION    How can you tell?

8. Save the captured traffic sample to a file called Ftpcapture.cap for future use.

## LAB REVIEW QUESTIONS

**Estimated completion time: 15 minutes**

1. How many subnets can you create with the network address supplied by your instructor (assuming that you can't use the all zeroes and all ones values)?

2. How many hosts can you create on each subnet with the network address supplied by your instructor?

3. How can you tell from the port numbers in a TCP traffic capture which computer initiated the connection sequence?

4. If you captured the same FTP traffic sample from Exercise 6-5 on a Token Ring network that supported frames up to 4500 bytes, how many Data Transfer To Client frames would be needed to send the Eula.txt file?

5. When capturing traffic on a Token Ring network supporting 4500-byte frames, how would the server know how large to make each segment?

6. How many Data Transfer To Client frames would be needed to transmit the Eula.txt file if a TCP implementation defaulted to the minimum segment size that a TCP/IP system can support (536 bytes)?

## LAB CHALLENGE 6-1: CALCULATING ADDITIONAL SUBNETS

**Estimated completion time: 15 minutes**

Using the subtraction method described in Chapter 5 of the textbook, calculate the IP address ranges for the next four subnets following the one that your instructor provided for this lab. Create a worksheet containing a copy of Table 6-2 for your answers. Do not use a calculator or any software to compute your answers.

**Table 6-2  Additional Subnet IP Addresses**

|  | Network Address | First IP Address | Last IP Address |
| --- | --- | --- | --- |
| First subnet |  |  |  |
| Second subnet |  |  |  |
| Third subnet |  |  |  |
| Fourth subnet |  |  |  |
| Fifth subnet |  |  |  |

# LAB CHALLENGE 6-2: ADVANCED DISPLAY FILTERING

**Estimated completion time: 15 minutes**

In Network Monitor in Computer*xx*, open the Ftpcapture.cap file you created in Exercise 6-6. To complete this challenge, you must create a display filter that causes Network Monitor to show only the frames specified in each of the following assignments:

1. Create a display filter that shows only the frames transferring part of the Eula.txt file from Server01 to Computer*xx*.

2. Create a display filter that shows all of the acknowledgment messages sent to Server01 by Computer*xx*.

3. Create a display filter that shows only the SYN and FIN frames for the FTP control connection.

> **NOTE** When adding an expression to a display filter, if a plus sign (+) appears next to a protocol, you can double-click the plus sign to expand the protocol and see a list of its properties. To modify the display filter decision tree, you can use the mouse to drag expressions and operators to different positions in the tree.

For each of the filters you create, take a screen shot (using ALT+PRNT SCRN) of the Display Filter dialog box, and then paste each of these screen shots into a separate WordPad document and name them LG*xx*Lab06-3.rtf, LG*xx*Lab06-4.rtf, and LG*xx*Lab06-5.rtf (where *xx* is the assigned number of your lab group). Your instructor will ask you to turn these in at the end of the lab.

## LAB 7
# TCP/IP

**This lab contains the following exercises and activities:**

■ Exercise 7-1: Configuring the Windows TCP/IP Client

■ Exercise 7-2: Testing Network Connections

■ Exercise 7-3: Configuring a Windows Router

■ Exercise 7-4: Testing the Router

■ Exercise 7-5: Capturing and Analyzing ICMP Traffic

■ Exercise 7-6: Installing RIP

■ Lab Review Questions

■ Lab Challenge 7-1: Creating Static Routes

## BEFORE YOU BEGIN

To complete this lab, you will need to obtain the following materials from your instructor:

■ The two-digit number assigned to your lab group. This number is used in the name of your lab group (LG*xx*, where *xx* is the number assigned to your group).

■ Table 6-1 from Lab 6 in this manual, in which you added the TCP/IP configuration parameters you computed for your lab group network.

■ A copy of the routing table from the Server01 server, supplied by your instructor.

**After completing this lab, you will be able to:**

■ Configure the Transmission Control Protocol/Internet Protocol (TCP/IP) client on a computer running Microsoft Windows Server 2003.

■ Configure a computer running Windows Server 2003 to function as a router.

■ Capture and analyze Internet Control Message Protocol (ICMP) traffic.

■ Install the Routing Information Protocol (RIP).

**Estimated lesson time:   135 minutes**

## SCENARIO

You are the new network administrator for Contoso, Ltd., a small company running a network with multiple computers running Windows Server 2003 and workstations running Microsoft Windows XP and Microsoft Windows 2000. Contoso has just acquired another small company and wants to assimilate that company's network into the Contoso network with a minimum of expense. To do this, you must configure one of the existing computers running Windows Server 2003 to function as a router between the original Contoso network and the new network.

## EXERCISE 7-1: CONFIGURING THE WINDOWS TCP/IP CLIENT

**Estimated completion time: 15 minutes**

In Lab 5 and Lab 6 of this manual, you calculated Internet Protocol (IP) addresses and a subnet mask for your lab group network, based on a network address assigned to you by your instructor. In this exercise you will configure your lab group computers to use those TCP/IP configuration settings.

1. Log on to Computer*xx* as Administrator, using the password **Pa$$w0rd**.

2. Open a Command Prompt window, and then type **ipconfig /all**.

> **QUESTION**   What is the current IP address and subnet mask for the Lab Group Network Connection interface?

3. Click Start, select Control Panel, select Network Connections, right-click Lab Group Network Connection, and then select Properties.

The Lab Group Network Connection Properties dialog box appears.

4. Select Internet Protocol (TCP/IP) from the components list, and then click Properties.

   The Internet Protocol (TCP/IP) Properties dialog box appears.

5. Select the Use The Following IP Address option.

6. In the IP Address text box, type the Computer*xx* IP address value from Table 6-1.

7. In the Subnet Mask text box, type the Subnet Mask value from Table 6-1.

   Leave the Default Gateway field and the DNS Server list empty.

8. Click OK to close the Internet Protocol (TCP/IP) Properties dialog box.

9. If a message box appears indicating that the local IP address will be configured as the primary DNS server address, click OK.

10. Click Close to close the Lab Group Network Connection Properties dialog box.

11. In the Command Prompt window, type **ipconfig /all** again.

> **QUESTION**   What is the IP address and subnet mask for the Lab Group Network Connection interface now?

12. Take a screen shot (using ALT+PRNT SCRN) of the Command Prompt window showing the Ipconfig display for the Lab Group Network Connection interface and then paste it into a WordPad document named LGxxLab07-1.rtf (where xx is the assigned number of your lab group).

    Your instructor will ask you to turn it in at the end of the lab.

13. Log on to Computeryy with the local Administrator account, using the password **Pa$$w0rd**.

14. Repeat steps 3–9 on Computeryy to configure its TCP/IP parameters, using the Computeryy IP address and subnet mask values from Table 6-1.

    On Computeryy, enter the Computerxx IP address value from Table 6-1 in the Default Gateway and Preferred DNS Server text boxes.

15. Leave the Command Prompt windows open on both computers for the next exercise.

## EXERCISE 7-2: TESTING NETWORK CONNECTIONS

**Estimated completion time: 15 minutes**

In this exercise you will test the network connections for your newly configured lab group network computers to determine their current communications capabilities.

1. In the Command Prompt window on Computerxx, type **route print** and then press ENTER.

**QUESTION**    How many entries are in Computerxx's routing table?

2. In the Command Prompt window, type **ping 10.1.100.1** and then press ENTER.

    **QUESTION**    What is the result?

    **QUESTION**    What does the result of this ping test prove?

3. In the Command Prompt window, type **ping**, followed by the IP address of Computeryy (from Table 6-1), and then press ENTER.

    **QUESTION**    What is the result of the test?

    **QUESTION**    What does this result prove?

4. In the Command Prompt window on Computeryy, use the Ping command to test connectivity to Computerxx.

    **QUESTION**    What is the command-line syntax you used to perform this test?

    **QUESTION**    What is the result of the test, and what does this result prove?

    **QUESTION**    Was it necessary to perform this last test? Why or why not?

5. Use Ping to test the connectivity between Computeryy and Server01.

**QUESTION**    What is the result of the test, and what does this result prove?

**QUESTION**    What must you add to the network for Computeryy to be able to communicate with Server01?

# EXERCISE 7-3: CONFIGURING A WINDOWS ROUTER

**Estimated completion time: 10 minutes**

In this exercise you will configure the Routing and Remote Access Service (RRAS) on Computerxx to route traffic between the Lab Group Network Connection interface and the Classroom Network Connection interface.

1.  On Computerxx, select Start, select Administrative Tools, and then select Routing And Remote Access.

    The Routing And Remote Access console appears.

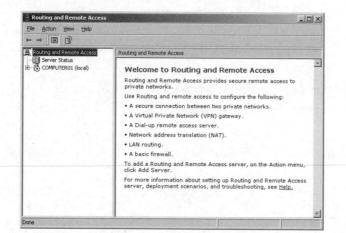

2.  In the console's scope pane (on the left), select the COMPUTERxx (local) icon and then select Configure And Enable Routing And Remote Access from the Action menu.

    The Routing And Remote Access Server Setup Wizard starts.

3.  Click Next to bypass the Welcome page.

    The Configuration page appears.

**4.** Select Custom Configuration, and then click Next.

The Custom Configuration page appears.

**5.** Select the LAN Routing check box, and then click Next.

The Completing The Routing And Remote Access Server Setup Wizard page appears.

**6.** Click Finish.

A Routing And Remote Access message box appears, asking if you want to start RRAS.

**7.** Click Yes.

RRAS starts.

8. Expand the COMPUTERxx (local) icon in the scope pane, and then select the Network Interfaces icon under the server icon.

**QUESTION**   Other than the default Loopback and Internal interfaces, what entries appear in the LAN And Demand Dial Interfaces list in the console's detail pane (on the right)?

9. Close the Routing And Remote Access console.

## EXERCISE 7-4: TESTING THE ROUTER

**Estimated completion time: 15 minutes**

In this exercise you will test the connectivity of Computeryy with the rest of the network. For this exercise your instructor will give you the routing table for the Server01 server on the classroom network.

**NOTE**   If you do not have an instructor to supply you with a routing table, use the following for Server01's routing table:

| Network Destination | Netmask | Gateway | Interface | Metric |
|---|---|---|---|---|
| 10.1.100.0 | 255.255.255.0 | 10.1.100.1 | 10.1.100.1 | 20 |
| 10.1.100.1 | 255.255.255.255 | 127.0.0.1 | 127.0.0.1 | 20 |
| 10.255.255.255 | 255.255.255.255 | 10.1.100.1 | 10.1.100.1 | 20 |
| 127.0.0.0 | 255.0.0.0 | 127.0.0.1 | 127.0.0.1 | 1 |
| 224.0.0.0 | 240.0.0.0 | 10.1.100.1 | 10.1.100.1 | 20 |
| 255.255.255.255 | 255.255.255.255 | 10.1.100.1 | 10.1.100.1 | 1 |

1. On Computeryy in the Command Prompt window, use the Ping command to test the computer's connectivity to the following destinations:

❑ Computerxx's Lab Group Network Connection IP address (from Table 6-1).

❑ Computerxx's Classroom Network Connection IP address. (See Exercise 3-2 in Lab 3 of this manual, or run **ipconfig /all** on Computerxx.)

❑ Server01's IP address (10.1.100.1).

> **QUESTION**    What are the results of these tests?

2. Based on the results of the ping tests you just performed, specify why each of the following possibilities can be ruled out as a cause of the failure you experienced.

> **QUESTION**    Computerxx has an incorrect default gateway address.

> **QUESTION**    Computeryy has an incorrect default gateway address.

> **QUESTION**    Computerxx is not routing traffic.

> **QUESTION**    Server01 is not configured to function as a router.

> **QUESTION**    Computerxx has an incorrectly configured routing table.

## EXERCISE 7-5: CAPTURING AND ANALYZING ICMP TRAFFIC

**Estimated completion time: 20 minutes**

In this exercise you will use Network Monitor to capture the ICMP traffic generated by your ping tests and use the information to determine why Computeryy can't communicate with the Server01 server.

1. Using Network Monitor on Computerxx, capture traffic first on the Lab Group Network Connection interface and then on the Classroom Network Connection interface, as you repeat the three ping tests you performed in Exercise 7-4.

> **NOTE**    *Opening Multiple Capture:# Summary Windows    To open multiple Capture: # Summary windows at the same time within Network Monitor, first capture the traffic on the Lab Group Network Connection interface and then display its Capture: # Summary window. Next, select Window, Lab Group Network Connection Capture*

Window (Session Stats). Switch to the Classroom Network Connection interface, capture its traffic, and then display its Capture: # Summary window.

Leave the Capture: # Summary windows for both captures open so you can refer to them later.

**2.** Create a display filter that causes Network Monitor to display only the frames containing ICMP traffic.

**3.** Take a screen shot (using ALT+PRNT SCRN) of the Microsoft Network Monitor window showing the ICMP messages you captured for the lab group network, and then paste it into a WordPad document named LG*xx*Lab07-2.rtf (where *xx* is the assigned number of your lab group) to turn in at the end of the lab.

**4.** Double-click one of the Echo frames you captured to display the Detail and Hex panes.

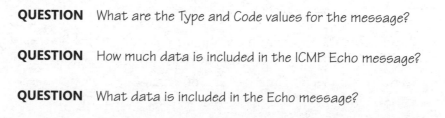

> **QUESTION**  What are the Type and Code values for the message?

> **QUESTION**  How much data is included in the ICMP Echo message?

> **QUESTION**  What data is included in the Echo message?

**5.** Based on the ICMP packets you captured using Network Monitor, answer the following questions.

**QUESTION**   Was Computeryy able to transmit ICMP messages to Computerxx?

**QUESTION**   Was Computeryy able to transmit ICMP messages to Server01?

**QUESTION**   Was Computerxx able to transmit ICMP response messages to Computeryy?

**QUESTION**   Was Server01 able to transmit ICMP response messages to Computeryy?

6. Open a Command Prompt window on both Computerxx and Computeryy and run the **route print** command in each one to display the routing tables for both computers.

7. Study the routing tables for Computerxx and Computeryy and compare them with the Server01 routing table supplied by your instructor.

**QUESTION**   What changes need to be made to prevent the ping failures from happening again?

# EXERCISE 7-6: INSTALLING RIP

**Estimated completion time: 20 minutes**

In this exercise you will install RIP on Computerxx so that it can communicate with the other RIP routers on the classroom network and update its routing table.

**NOTE   RIP and Server01**   Your instructor has already installed and configured RIP on the Server01 server, enabling the lab group servers in the classroom to share their routing tables with Server01 as well.

1. On Computerxx, open the Routing And Remote Access console.

2. In the console's scope pane, expand the IP Routing icon under the icon for your server.

3. Select General, and then select New Routing Protocol from the Action menu.

The New Routing Protocol dialog box appears.

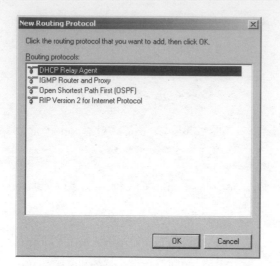

4. Select RIP Version 2 For Internet Protocol, and then click OK.

   The RIP icon appears in the scope pane.

5. Select the RIP icon, and then select New Interface from the Action menu.

   The New Interface For RIP Version 2 For Internet Protocol dialog box appears.

**New Interface for RIP Version 2 for Internet Protocol**

This routing protocol runs on the interface that you select below.

Interfaces:

Classroom Network Connection
Lab Group Network Connection

OK          Cancel

**6.** Select Classroom Network Connection, and then click OK.

The RIP Properties dialog box appears.

**RIP Properties - Classroom Network Connection Properties**

General | Security | Neighbors | Advanced

Routing Information Protocol (RIP) Interface

Operation mode:
Periodic update mode

Outgoing packet protocol:
RIP version 2 broadcast

Incoming packet protocol:
RIP version 1 and 2

Added cost for routes:    1

Tag for announced routes:    0

☐ Activate authentication

Password:

OK          Cancel          Apply

**7.** Click OK to close the RIP Properties dialog box.

**8.** With the RIP icon selected in the left pane of the console, select Refresh from the Action menu.

If the Responses Sent and Responses Received columns still have values of 0, wait a few minutes and then refresh the display again until values greater than 0 appear.

**9.** Take a screen shot (using ALT+PRNT SCRN) of the Routing And Remote Access console showing non-zero values for the Responses Sent and

Responses Received columns and then paste it into a WordPad document named LG*xx*Lab07-3.rtf (where *xx* is the assigned number of your lab group).

Your instructor will ask you to turn it in at the end of the lab.

10. On Computer*yy*, repeat the three ping tests from step 1 of Exercise 7-4.

> **QUESTION**    What change do you see in the test results?

> **QUESTION**    Why did the results change?

11. In the Command Prompt window on Computer*xx*, run the **route print** command again.

> **QUESTION**    How many entries are in Computer*xx*'s routing table now?

12. Ask some of the students in other lab groups for the IP addresses of their Computer*yy* computers, and try to ping them from your Computer*yy*.

> **QUESTION**    Were you successful?

13. After allowing RIP time to update the routing table on Computer*xx* with entries for all of the other lab group networks in the classroom, display the routing table in the Command Prompt window.

14. Take a screen shot (using ALT+PRNT SCRN) of the routing table, and then paste it into a WordPad document named LG*xx*Lab07-4.rtf (where *xx* is the assigned number of your lab group).

Your instructor will ask you to turn it in at the end of the lab.

15. Close the Routing And Remote Access console and Network Monitor on Computer*xx* and the Command Prompt windows on both computers. Then log off both computers.

## LAB REVIEW QUESTIONS

**Estimated completion time: 15 minutes**

1. In Exercise 7-2, why was Computer*yy* able to communicate with Computer*xx* but not with Server01?

2.  In Exercise 7-2, why was Computerxx able to communicate with both Computeryy and Server01?

3.  How can you account for the difference in the number of entries in Computerxx's routing table in Exercise 7-2 and Exercise 7-6?

4.  Assuming that you never installed RIP, what Route.exe command line would you use to ensure the success of all the ping tests from Exercise 7-4? Which computer would you run it on?

5.  In Exercise 7-5, how were you able to determine why Computeryy could not ping the Server01 server on the classroom network?

# LAB CHALLENGE 7-1: CREATING STATIC ROUTES

**Estimated completion time: 20 minutes**

1.  On Computerxx, disable RIP by deleting the RIP protocol module in the Routing And Remote Access console.

2.  Using Route.exe and the screen shot of Computerxx's routing table you took in Exercise 7-6, delete all of the entries for the other lab group networks in the classroom from Computerxx's routing table.

3.  Re-create the routing table entries for all of the other lab group networks manually by creating static routes in the Routing And Remote Access console.

4.  Ping the Computeryy computer on each of the other lab groups from your lab group Computeryy to ensure that your routes are correct.

5.  Take a screen shot (using ALT+PRNT SCRN) of the Static Routes list in the Routing And Remote Access console and then paste it into a Word-Pad document named LGxxLab07-5.rtf (where xx is the assigned number of your lab group).

Your instructor will ask you to turn it in at the end of the lab.

# TROUBLESHOOTING LAB A:
# TCP/IP CONFIGURATION

Troubleshooting Lab A is a practical application of the knowledge you have acquired from Labs 1 through 7. Your instructor or lab assistant has changed your computer configuration, causing it to "break." Your task in this lab will be to apply your acquired skills to troubleshoot and resolve the break. Two scenarios are presented that lay out the parameters of the breaks and the conditions that must be met for the scenarios to be resolved. The first break scenario involves Transmission Control Protocol/Internet Protocol (TCP/IP) configuration on a computer with one network interface, and the second break scenario involves TCP/IP configuration on a multihomed computer.

> **CAUTION**  Do not proceed with this lab until you receive guidance from your instructor.
>
> Your instructor will inform you which break scenario you will be performing (Break Scenario 1 or Break Scenario 2) and which computer to use. Your instructor or lab assistant might also have special instructions. Consult with your instructor before proceeding.

## Break Scenario 1

Freeman, a new hire at Contoso, Ltd., is having trouble connecting to the company network, so he calls the help desk, where you are working the night shift. Freeman was issued a new computer, called Computeryy, and assured his supervisor that he could configure it himself. The supervisor provided Freeman with an Internet Protocol (IP) address, a subnet mask, and a Domain Name System (DNS) server address. However, after configuring the TCP/IP client on the computer, Freeman is still unable to access the network, and he asks you to come over and help him.

Troubleshoot Computeryy until you're able to ping Computerxx successfully. You can view the configuration of Computerxx, but you can't change any of its settings.

As you resolve the problem, fill out the worksheet in the Lab Manual\TroubleshootingLabA folder and include the following information:

- A description of the problem

- A list of all steps taken to diagnose the problem, even the ones that didn't work

- A description of the exact issue and solution

- A list of the tools and resources you used to help solve this problem

## Break Scenario 2

You are a network support specialist working the help desk at Blue Yonder Airlines when a call comes in from the manager of the Research and Development (R&D) division. The R&D division has just deployed a new local area network (LAN) for its own projects and has installed a Microsoft Windows Server 2003 computer to function as the router between the R&D network and the company's main backbone network. The router computer is called Computerxx. The workstations on the R&D network are capable of communicating among themselves, but they can't communicate with Computerxx or with any other networks, including the backbone. The R&D manager wants you to come and troubleshoot the problem.

At the site of the R&D network you have access to Computerxx and to a workstation on the R&D network called Computeryy. After checking the physical network connections on the computers and the configuration of the Routing and Remote Access Service (RRAS) on Computerxx, you begin to suspect that there is a TCP/IP configuration problem. The backbone network has a Dynamic Host Configuration Protocol (DHCP) server on it that supplies IP addresses and other TCP/IP configuration parameters to all the computers connected to the backbone. The new R&D network uses static IP addresses based on a network address supplied by the company's Information Technology (IT) division.

Assuming that the network hardware and the RRAS configuration are both intact and correct, troubleshoot the computers until Computerxx is able to communicate with both the backbone network and the R&D network.

As you resolve the problem, fill out the worksheet in the Lab Manual\TroubleshootingLabA folder and include the following information:

- A description of the problem

- A list of all steps taken to diagnose the problem, even the ones that didn't work

- A description of the exact issue and solution

- A list of the tools and resources you used to help solve this problem

## LAB 8
# NETWORKING SOFTWARE

**This lab contains the following exercises and activities:**

- Exercise 8-1: Examining DNS Information

- Exercise 8-2: Installing a DHCP Server

- Exercise 8-3: Configuring a DHCP Server

- Exercise 8-4: Monitoring DHCP

- Exercise 8-5: Configuring Linux for Windows Access

- Exercise 8-6: Accessing a Linux Server from Windows

- Lab Review Questions

- Lab Challenge 8-1: Creating Additional Scopes

- Lab Challenge 8-2: Creating Reverse Lookup Zones

## BEFORE YOU BEGIN

To complete this lab, you will need to get the following materials from your instructor:

- The two-digit number assigned to your lab group. This number is used in the name of your group (LG*xx*, where *xx* is the number assigned to your lab group).

- Table 6-1 from Lab 6 of this manual, in which you added the Transmission Control Protocol/Internet Protocol (TCP/IP) configuration parameters you computed for your lab group network.

- The network address, unique to your lab group, assigned by your instructor in Lab 5 of this manual.

**After completing this lab, you will be able to:**

- Install and configure a Dynamic Host Configuration Protocol (DHCP) server.
- Analyze DHCP traffic.
- Examine Domain Name System (DNS) resource record information.
- Create a user account on a Linux system.
- Access a Linux server from a system running Microsoft Windows.

**Estimated lesson time:    135 minutes**

## SCENARIO

As the new network administrator for Contoso, Ltd., you are surprised to discover that all the computers had statically configured Internet Protocol (IP) addresses. From talking to the users, you find out that duplicate address errors occur frequently and that users often waste a lot of time waiting for a network support representative to fix the problem. To streamline the IP address allocation procedures for the company network, you decide to install a DHCP server and have all client computers use it to obtain their Transmission Control Protocol/Internet Protocol (TCP/IP) configuration settings.

## EXERCISE 8-1: EXAMINING DNS INFORMATION

**Estimated completion time: 10 minutes**

In this exercise, you will examine the information stored in the DNS server running on your lab group Computer*xx*, which was installed and configured when you installed the Active Directory directory service on the server in Lab 4 of this manual. You will use this information later in this lab.

1. Log on to Computer*xx* as Administrator, using the password **Pa$$w0rd**.

2. Click Start, select Administrative Tools, and then select DNS.

   The Dnsmgmt console appears.

3. In the console's scope pane, expand the Forward Lookup Zones folder, and then select the lgxx.contoso.com zone folder (where *xx* is the number of your lab group assigned by your instructor).

4. Examine the resource records in the zone and write down the contents of the Host records for the computers in your lab group in a table like the following:

| Host Name | IP Address |
|---|---|
|  |  |
|  |  |
|  |  |
|  |  |

> **QUESTION**   How many Host records are there for the computers in your lab group?

5. Take a screen shot (using ALT+PRNT SCRN) of the Dnsmgmt console with the contents of the lgxx.contoso.com zone displayed, and then paste it into a WordPad document named LGxxLab08-1.rtf (where *xx* is the assigned number of your lab group).

   Your instructor will ask you to turn it in at the end of the lab.

6. Close the Dnsmgmt console.

# EXERCISE 8-2: INSTALLING A DHCP SERVER

**Estimated completion time: 15 minutes**

In Lab 6 of this manual, you calculated a range of IP addresses for your lab group network. In this exercise you will install and authorize the DHCP service on Computerxx so that the server can deploy those addresses as needed.

1. On Computerxx, click Start, select Control Panel, and then select Add Or Remove Programs.

    The Add Or Remove Programs window appears.

2. Click the Add/Remove Windows Components button on the left.

    The Windows Components Wizard page appears.

3. In the Components box, scroll down and select Networking Services, and then click Details.

    The Networking Services dialog box appears.

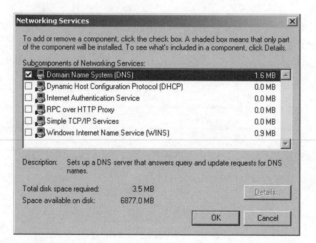

4. In the Networking Services box, select the Dynamic Host Configuration Protocol (DHCP) check box, and then click OK.

    The Windows Components page reappears.

5. Click Next.

    The Configuring Components page shows a progress indicator as the changes you requested are made. If you are prompted to insert the Windows Server 2003 installation CD, click OK and navigate to the C:\Win2k3\I386 folder. The Completing The Windows Components Wizard page appears.

6. Click Finish.

7. Close the Add Or Remove Programs window.

8. Click the Start menu, select Administrative Tools, and then select DHCP.

   The DHCP console appears and computer*xx*.lg*xx*.contoso.com is listed in the scope pane (where *xx* is the number of your lab group).

9. In the scope pane, expand the computer*xx*.lg*xx*.contoso.com icon.

   A red down-arrow appears to the left of the server name.

10. Click computer*xx*.lg*xx*.contoso.com and then select Authorize from the Action menu.

    The red down-arrow remains until you refresh the display. Leave the DHCP console open for the next exercise.

## EXERCISE 8-3: CONFIGURING A DHCP SERVER

**Estimated completion time: 20 minutes**

In this exercise, you will create a DHCP scope on Computer*xx* and configure the DHCP options that the server will supply with the IP addresses.

1. In the DHCP console on Computer*xx*, verify that computer*xx*.lg*xx*.contoso.com is highlighted, and then select New Scope from the Action menu.

   The New Scope Wizard appears.

2. Click Next.

   The Scope Name page appears.

**3.** In the Name text box, type **LGxx Network** (where *xx* is the number assigned to your lab group by your instructor), and then click Next.

The IP Address Range page appears.

**4.** Type the Computer*xx* IP address value from Table 6-1 in the Start IP Address text box and type the last IP address value in the End IP Address text box.

The console automatically adds a value to the Subnet Mask text box.

> **QUESTION**   Where did the console obtain this Subnet Mask value?

> **QUESTION**   Is the automatically supplied Subnet Mask value correct for your network? Why or why not?

**5.** In the Subnet Mask text box, type the Subnet Mask value from Table 6-1, and then click your cursor in the Length box.

> **QUESTION**   The value in the Length box should now match the value of the number following the slash in the network address supplied to you by your instructor. Why is this so?

**6.** Click Next.

The Add Exclusions page appears.

**7.** In the Start IP Address text box, type the Computer*xx* IP address value from Table 6-1, type the Computer*yy* IP Address value from Table 6-1 in the End Address text box, and then click Add.

The values you entered now appear in the Excluded Address Range box.

**QUESTION**   Why was it necessary to exclude these addresses?

**8.** Click Next.

The Lease Duration page appears. Notice that the default lease duration is eight days.

**9.** In the Days box, type **365**. Then click Next.

The Configure DHCP Options page appears, asking if you would like to configure the most common DHCP options now.

**10.** Verify that the Yes, I Want To Configure These Options Now option is selected, and then click Next.

The Router (Default Gateway) page appears.

**11.** In the IP Address text box, type the Computer*xx* IP address value from Table 6-1, and then click Add.

The address you entered appears in the list of routers.

**12.** Click Next.

The Domain Name And DNS Server page appears.

**13.** In the Server Name text box, type **Computer*xx***, and then click Resolve.

   **QUESTION**   What happens?

**14.** Click Add to add the address to the list of DNS servers, and then click Next.

**15.** Click Next to bypass the WINS Servers page.

The Activate Scope page appears.

**16.** Click Next to accept the default Yes, I Want To Activate This Scope Now option.

The Completing The New Scope Wizard page appears.

**17.** Click Finish.

An icon representing the new scope appears in the DHCP console. Notice that computer*xx*.lg*xx*.contoso.com now contains a green up-arrow. This appears because you have authorized Computer*xx* and created a scope.

18. Click the computer*xx*.lg*xx*.contoso.com icon in the scope pane, take a screen shot (using ALT+PRNT SCRN) of the DHCP console, and then paste it into a WordPad document named LG*xx*Lab08-2.rtf (where *xx* is the assigned number of your lab group).

Your instructor will ask you to turn it in at the end of the lab.

19. Leave the DHCP console open for the next exercise.

## EXERCISE 8-4: MONITORING DHCP

**Estimated completion time: 15 minutes**

In this exercise, you will configure Computer*yy* to obtain its IP address and other TCP/IP configuration settings from the DHCP service you installed on Computer*xx*. You will also monitor the effects of the process on network traffic and on the DNS server.

1. On Computer*xx*, open Network Monitor and configure the program to capture traffic from the computer's Lab Group Network Connection interface.

2. From the Capture menu, select Start to begin capturing network data.

3. Log on to Computer*yy* with the local Administrator account, using the password **Pa$$w0rd**.

4. Open the Local Area Connection Properties and Internet Protocol (TCP/IP) Properties dialog boxes, select the Obtain An IP Address Automatically and Obtain DNS Server Address Automatically options, and then click OK to close both boxes.

5. Restart Computer*yy*.

6. When the Welcome To Windows screen appears on Computer*yy*, select Stop And View from the Capture menu in Network Monitor on Computer*xx*.

7. In Network Monitor, create a display filter that causes the program to show only the DHCP frames in the traffic sample you captured.

> **QUESTION**   What DHCP message types do you see in the capture summary?

> **QUESTION**   How many times did Computer*yy* transmit a request for an IP address?

**QUESTION**  How can you tell?

**QUESTION**  Which of the DHCP packets you captured contains the IP address that the Computerxx assigned to Computeryy?

**QUESTION**  What IP address did DHCP assign to Computeryy?

8. Take a screen shot (using ALT+PRNT SCRN) of the Microsoft Network Monitor window with the captured DHCP messages displayed, and then paste it into a WordPad document named LGxxLab08-3.rtf (where xx is the assigned number of your lab group).

   Your instructor will ask you to turn it in at the end of the lab.

9. Close Network Monitor without saving the capture.

10. Open the Dnsmgmt console on Computerxx again, look in the lgxx.contoso.com zone, and examine the Host resource records for your lab group servers.

**QUESTION**  What has changed since you examined these records?

# EXERCISE 8-5: CONFIGURING LINUX FOR WINDOWS ACCESS

**Estimated completion time: 20 minutes**

In this exercise, you will create a user account for yourself on the LinuxServer01 computer and configure the Linux system to function as a server, accessible from Computerxx.

1. Log on to the LinuxServer01 server on the classroom network with the user name root and the password **Pa$$w0rd**.

   **NOTE  Using the Root Account**  In Linux and UNIX, the user name "root" is the equivalent of the default Administrator account on a computer running Windows. Logging on as root gives you full access to all areas of the operating system.

2. Click the Red Hat icon on the taskbar, select System Settings, and then select Users And Groups.

The Red Hat User Manager window appears.

3. Click Add User.

   The Create New User dialog box appears.

4. In the User Name field, type the name you want to use for your user account. Use only lowercase letters in the name.

5. In the Full Name field, type your first and last names.

6. In the Password and Confirm Password fields, type a password (at least six characters long) for your account.

   **QUESTION**   *What path name appears in the Home Directory text box?*

7. Click OK.

   **QUESTION**   *What happens?*

**8.** Close the User Manager window.

**9.** Click the Red Hat icon, select System Settings, select Server Settings, and then select Samba.

The Samba Server Configuration dialog box appears.

**10.** Click Add.

The Create Samba Share dialog box appears.

**11.** In the Directory text box, type the home directory path name that appeared earlier when you created your user account.

**12.** Under Basic Permissions, select the Read/Write option.

**13.** Select the Access tab and select the Allow Access To Everyone option. Then click OK.

The shared home directory appears in the Samba Server Configuration window.

**14.** From the Preferences menu, select Samba Users.

The Samba Users dialog box appears.

**15.** Click Add User.

The Create New Samba User dialog box appears.

**16.** In the UNIX Username list, select the name of the account you just created.

**17.** In the Windows User Name text box, type **Administrator**.

**18.** In the Samba Password and Confirm Samba Password text boxes, type the same password you assigned to your user account earlier.

**19.** Click OK.

> **QUESTION**   What happens?

**20.** Click OK.

**21.** Log off the LinuxServer01 computer.

## EXERCISE 8-6: ACCESSING A LINUX SERVER FROM WINDOWS

**Estimated completion time: 10 minutes**

In this exercise, you will access the LinuxServer01 server on the classroom network from Computer*xx*, using the account you created in Exercise 8-5.

> **NOTE   Expect Delays**   It might take some time for the changes you made in Exercise 8-5 to take effect and for the LinuxServer01 computer to appear on the network. If you can't access the Linux system from Windows right away, wait at least 10 minutes and try again.

**1.** On Computer*xx*, launch Windows Explorer.

**2.** Expand the My Network Places entry in the scope pane and browse to the Linux  workgroup under Microsoft Windows Network.

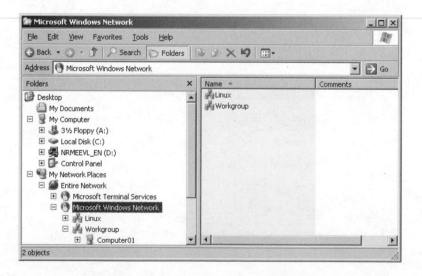

> **QUESTION**   What systems appear in the Linux workgroup?

3. Double-click the LinuxServer01 icon.

The Connect To LinuxServer01 dialog box appears.

Connect to linuxclass01.contoso.com    ? X

Connecting to Linuxclass01

User name:    🔒    ▼

Password:    

☐ Remember my password

OK    Cancel

4. In the User Name and Password text boxes, type the name and password for the user you created on LinuxServer01 in Exercise 8-5 and then click OK.

**QUESTION**  What happens?

5. Double-click the share you created in your user's home directory.

**QUESTION**  What are the contents of that home directory?

6. Copy the Eula.txt file from the C:\Windist\i386 folder on Computerxx to the home directory on LinuxServer01.

7. Take a screen shot (using ALT+PRNT SCRN) of Windows Explorer showing the contents of the home directory, including the Eula.txt file you just copied there, and then paste it into a WordPad document named LGxxLab08-4.rtf (where xx is the assigned number of your lab group).

Your instructor will ask you to turn it in at the end of the lab.

8. Close Windows Explorer.

# LAB REVIEW QUESTIONS

**Estimated completion time: 15 minutes**

1. On an actual production network, why would it typically be necessary to configure the DHCP Router option as a scope option and the DNS Servers option as a server option?

2. What would happen if you failed to activate the scope you created in Exercise 8-3 before you restarted Computeryy?

3. What would happen if you shut down the DHCP service on Computerxx and then restarted Computeryy?

4. Apart from examining the captured traffic in Network Monitor, list two ways that you can tell what IP address was assigned to Computeryy by the DHCP Server service running on Computerxx.

## LAB CHALLENGE 8-1: CREATING ADDITIONAL SCOPES

**Estimated completion time: 15 minutes**

In Lab Challenge 6-1 in Lab 6 of this manual, you calculated IP address ranges for the subnets following the one assigned to your lab group and recorded the addresses in Table 6-2. To complete this lab challenge, create a DHCP scope on Computerxx for each of the subnets in Table 6-1. Then take a screen shot (using ALT+PRNT SCRN) of the DHCP console displaying the scopes and paste it into a WordPad document named LGxxLab08-5.rtf (where xx is the assigned number of your lab group). Your instructor will ask you to turn it in at the end of the lab.

## LAB CHALLENGE 8-2: CREATING REVERSE LOOKUP ZONES

**Estimated completion time: 15 minutes**

The DNS Server service was automatically installed on Computerxx when you installed Active Directory in Lab 4 of this manual. During that installation, Windows Server 2003 created a forward lookup zone for your new domain, but it did not create a reverse lookup zone. To complete this challenge, do the following:

1. Create a reverse lookup zone for your lab group domain, using the IP addresses you calculated in Lab 6 of this manual.

2. Populate the new zone with Pointer records for the computers in your lab group, using their current IP addresses.

3. Take a screen shot (using ALT+PRNT SCRN) of the Dnsmgmt console displaying the reverse lookup zone and its contents and paste it into a WordPad document named LGxxLab08-6.rtf (where xx is the assigned number of your lab group).

Your instructor will ask you to turn it in at the end of the lab.

# TROUBLESHOOTING DHCP

Troubleshooting Lab B is a practical application of the knowledge you have acquired from Labs 1 through 8. Your instructor or lab assistant has changed your computer configuration, causing it to "break." Your task in this lab will be to apply your acquired skills to troubleshoot and resolve the break. Two scenarios are presented that lay out the parameters of the breaks and the conditions that must be met for the scenarios to be resolved. In this lab both break scenarios involve the Dynamic Host Configuration Protocol (DHCP).

> **CAUTION**  Do not proceed with this lab until you receive guidance from your instructor.
>
> Your instructor will inform you which break scenario you will be performing (Break Scenario 1 or Break Scenario 2) and which computer to use. Your instructor or lab assistant might also have special instructions. Consult with your instructor before proceeding.

## Break Scenario 1

Mary Ann, an employee of Blue Yonder Airlines, turned on her computer this morning and discovered that although she could run her usual word processing program, she could not retrieve her e-mail or access the Internet. So she called the help desk and you answered the phone. Mary Ann's computer is on a network equipped with a DHCP server that supplies Internet Protocol (IP) addresses and other Transmission Control Protocol/Internet Protocol (TCP/IP) configuration settings to all connected systems. The computer running the DHCP server is called Computerxx, and Mary Ann's computer is called Computeryy.

Troubleshoot Mary Ann's computer and the DHCP server until Mary Ann can access network resources such as the Internet and her e-mail.

As you resolve the problem, fill out the worksheet in the Lab Manual\TroubleshootingLabB folder and include the following information:

- A description of the problem

- A list of all steps taken to diagnose the problem, even the ones that didn't work

- A description of the exact issue and solution

- A list of the tools and resources you used to help solve this problem

## Break Scenario 2

Harold turned his computer on this morning and found that he was unable to connect to the company network or the Internet. On checking his computer's TCP/IP configuration with Ipconfig.exe, he noticed that his IP address was 169.254.0.1, which is not an address in the subnet to which Harold's computer is connected. Puzzled, Harold called the help desk and your supervisor has sent you to troubleshoot the problem. Harold's computer is called Computeryy and the DHCP server is called Computerxx. Troubleshoot these two computers until Harold's computer successfully obtains an IP address from Computerxx.

As you resolve the problem, fill out the worksheet in the Lab Manual\TroubleshootingLabB folder and include the following information:

- A description of the problem

- A list of all steps taken to diagnose the problem, even the ones that didn't work

- A description of the exact issue and solution

- A list of the tools and resources you used to help solve this problem

# NETWORK SECURITY AND AVAILABILITY

**This lab contains the following exercises and activities:**

- Exercise 9-1: Preparing the Web Server

- Exercise 9-2: Configuring TCP/IP Packet Filters

- Exercise 9-3: Configuring RRAS Packet Filters

- Exercise 9-4: Resetting RRAS

- Exercise 9-5: Installing a NAT Router

- Exercise 9-6: Demonstrating NAT

- Lab Review Questions

- Lab Challenge 9-1: Reversing the NAT Configuration

## BEFORE YOU BEGIN

To complete this lab, you will need to obtain the following information from your instructor:

- The two-digit number assigned to your lab group. This number is used in the name of your lab group (LG*xx*, where *xx* is the number assigned to your group).

- Table 6-1 from Lab 6, in which you added the TCP/IP configuration parameters you computed for your lab group network.

## SCENARIO

Contoso, Ltd. has a Research and Development (R&D) department that operates its own network but still requires access to resources on the main company network. To provide a protected environment for the R&D users, you decide to use packet filters to restrict the types of traffic permitted on the network and to install NAT on the Microsoft Windows router that connects the R&D network to the company network.

### After completing this lab, you will be able to:

- Configure packet filters on a Microsoft Windows Transmission Control Protocol/ Internet Protocol (TCP/IP) client.
- Configure packet filters in the Routing and Remote Access Service (RRAS).
- Install and configure a Windows Network Address Translation (NAT) server.

**Estimated lesson time:   145 minutes**

## EXERCISE 9-1: PREPARING THE WEB SERVER

**Estimated completion time: 10 minutes**

In this exercise, you will create a home page for the Web server running on your lab group Computeryy, which will represent the content you want to protect from unauthorized access.

1. On Computeryy, log on using the local Administrator account, using the password **Pa$$w0rd**.

2. Click Start, select All Programs, select Accessories, and then select Notepad.

   The Notepad window appears.

3. In the Notepad window, type the following:

```
<HTML>
<TITLE>W A R N I N G !</TITLE>
<BODY BGCOLOR="FF0000">
<H1>WARNING!</H1>
<H2>You have accessed a secured page on a server belonging to lab group
LGxx. Terminate this connection immediately or be prepared to face
departmental sanctions including loss of pay and termination of
employment.</H2>
</BODY>
</HTML>
```

4. Replace the *xx* in the code listing with the number assigned to your lab group by your administrator.

5. From the File menu, select Save As, and then save the file as **Default.htm** in the C:\Inetpub\Wwwroot folder on Computeryy.

6. Close Notepad.

7. Click Start, select All Programs, and then select Internet Explorer.

   The Internet Explorer window appears.

8. In the Address text box, type **localhost** and then press ENTER.

   **QUESTION**   What is the result?

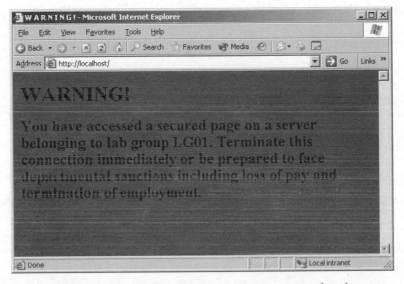

9. From a computer in one of the other lab groups in the classroom, open Internet Explorer. In the Address box, type **http://** plus the Internet Protocol (IP) address of your Computeryy computer (as you recorded it in Table 6-1), and then press ENTER.

   **QUESTION**   What is the result?

# EXERCISE 9-2: CONFIGURING TCP/IP PACKET FILTERS

**Estimated completion time: 20 minutes**

In this exercise, you will configure the TCP/IP client on Computeryy to filter packets based on Transmission Control Protocol (TCP) port numbers. This enables you to limit user access to the system.

1. On Computeryy, click Start, select Control Panel, and then select Network Connections; then right-click the Local Area Connection interface; and then select Properties.

   The Local Area Connection Properties dialog box appears.

2. Select Internet Protocol (TCP/IP), and then click Properties.

   The Internet Protocol (TCP/IP) Properties dialog box appears.

3. Click Advanced.

   The Advanced TCP/IP Settings dialog box appears.

4. Click the Options tab, and then click Properties.

   The TCP/IP Filtering dialog box appears.

5. Select the Enable TCP/IP Filtering (All Adapters) check box.

**6.** In the TCP Ports column, select Permit Only.

**7.** Click Add.

The Add Filter dialog box appears.

**8.** Type **80** in the TCP Port text box, and then click OK.

> **QUESTION** What service does the well-known port number 80 represent?

**9.** Take a screen shot (using ALT+PRNT SCRN) of the TCP/IP Filtering dialog box, and then paste it into a WordPad document named LGxxLab9-1.rtf (where xx is the assigned number of your lab group).

Your instructor will ask you to turn it in at the end of the lab.

**10.** Click OK to close the TCP/IP Filtering dialog box.

**11.** Click OK to close the Advanced TCP/IP Settings dialog box.

**12.** Click OK to close the Internet Protocol (TCP/IP) Properties dialog box.

**13.** Click Close to close the Local Area Connection Properties dialog box.

A Local Network message box appears, stating that you must restart the computer for the new settings to take effect.

14. Click Yes to restart the computer.

15. After Computeryy restarts on Computerxx, log on as Administrator, using the password **Pa$$w0rd**.

16. Launch Microsoft Internet Explorer and in the Address text box, type **http**:// plus Computeryy's IP address, and then click Go.

> **QUESTION**   *What happens?*

17. In the Address text box, type **ftp**:// plus Computeryy's IP address, and then click Go.

> **QUESTION**   *What happens now? Explain the reason for what happens.*

18. After you have completed the test, open the TCP/IP Filtering dialog box on Computeryy again, and then disable TCP/IP Filtering.

19. Close the TCP/IP Filtering dialog box, and then restart Computeryy.

## EXERCISE 9-3: CONFIGURING RRAS PACKET FILTERS

**Estimated completion time: 20 minutes**

In this exercise, you will again create packet filters, this time on your Computerxx, and using the Routing And Remote Access console instead of the TCP/IP client.

1. On Computerxx, click Start, select Administrative Tools, and then select Routing And Remote Access to open the Routing And Remote Access console.

2. Expand the icon representing your server in the left pane, and then expand the IP Routing icon.

3. Select the General icon in the left pane.

A list of network interfaces appears in the details pane.

4. Select the Lab Group Network Connection interface in the right pane, and then select Properties from the Action menu.

The Lab Group Network Connection Properties dialog box appears.

5. Click Outbound Filters.

The Outbound Filters dialog box appears.

**Outbound Filters**

These filters control which packets are received by this network.

Filter action:

( ) Transmit all packets except those that meet the criteria below

( ) Drop all packets except those that meet the criteria below

Filters:

| Source Address | Source Network Mask | Destination Address | Destination Mask | P |
|---|---|---|---|---|
| | | | | |

[ New... ]  [ Edit... ]  [ Delete ]

[ OK ]  [ Cancel ]

**6.** Click New.

The Add IP Filter dialog box appears.

**Add IP Filter**

[ ] Source network

IP address: _____

Subnet mask: _____

[ ] Destination network

IP address: _____

Subnet mask: _____

Protocol: [ Any ▼ ]

[ OK ]  [ Cancel ]

**7.** From the Protocol drop-down list, select TCP.

**8.** Leave the Source Port text box blank, type **80** in the Destination Port text box, and then click OK to close the Add IP Filter dialog box.

**9.** Take a screen shot (using ALT+PRNT SCRN) of the Outbound Filters dialog box, and then paste it into a WordPad document named LGxxLab9-2.rtf (where xx is the assigned number of your lab group).

Your instructor will ask you to turn it in at the end of the lab.

10. Click OK twice to close the Outbound Filters dialog box and the Lab Group Network Connection Properties dialog box.

11. From another lab group's computer in the classroom, open a Command Prompt window; then at the command prompt, type **ping** plus the IP address of your lab group's Computeryy; and then press ENTER.

    **QUESTION**   What is the result? Why?

    **NOTE   Clearing the Browser Cache**   If you are working at the same computer you used to test the Web server connection in Exercise 9-1, be sure to clear Internet Explorer's browser cache before you perform step 12. You can do this by selecting Internet Options from the Tools menu, clicking the Delete Files button, and then clicking OK in the Delete Files dialog box.

12. On the same computer in another lab group, open Internet Explorer. In the Address box, type **http://** plus the IP address of your Computeryy computer, and press ENTER.

    **QUESTION**   What is the result? Why?

13. On Computerxx, open the Outbound Filters dialog box for the Lab Group Network Connection again, select the Drop All Packets Except Those That Meet The Criteria Below option, and then click OK twice.

14. Repeat the ping and browser tests you performed in steps 11 and 12 (remembering to clear the browser cache again).

    **QUESTION**   What are the results now? Why?

## EXERCISE 9-4: RESETTING RRAS

**Estimated completion time: 5 minutes**

In this exercise, you will remove the RRAS configuration you created in Lab 7. You can use this same procedure at any time to return RRAS to its default state.

    **NOTE   Removing the RRAS Configuration**   When you reset RRAS using this procedure, all configuration settings are lost.

1. If necessary, on Computerxx, open the Routing And Remote Access console.

2. In the console's scope pane, select the COMPUTERxx (local) icon.

3. From the Action menu, select Disable Routing And Remote Access.

   A Routing And Remote Access message box appears, warning that you are about to disable the router.

4. Click Yes.

   RRAS returns to its default unconfigured state.

## EXERCISE 9-5: INSTALLING A NAT ROUTER

**Estimated completion time: 15 minutes**

In this exercise, you will configure RRAS to function as a Network Address Translation (NAT) router so that the computers on the lab group network are inaccessible from the classroom network but can still access the classroom network as needed.

1. In the Routing And Remote Access console on Computerxx, from the Action menu, select Configure And Enable Routing And Remote Access.

   The Routing And Remote Access Server Setup Wizard appears.

2. Click Next to bypass the Welcome page.

   The Configuration page appears.

3. Select the Network Address Translation (NAT) option, and then click Next.

The NAT Internet Connection page appears.

4. Make sure the Use This Public Interface To Connect To The Internet option is selected, select Classroom Network Connection in the list of interfaces, and then click Next.

   The Completing The Routing And Remote Access Server Setup Wizard page appears.

5. Click Finish to configure and start RRAS.

   **QUESTION** For the purposes of this lab, both the networks to which Computerxx is connected use unregistered IP addresses. However, when NAT is used to provide Internet connectivity, which of the router's two interfaces must use a registered IP address?

6. Expand the COMPUTERxx (local) icon and the IP Routing icon, and then examine the various elements of the Routing And Remote Access console interface.

   **QUESTION** How does the Routing And Remote Access console interface for the NAT router configuration differ from that of the local area network (LAN) router configuration you created in Lab 7?

7. Take a screen shot (using ALT+PRNT SCRN) of the Routing And Remote Access console that best illustrates the difference between the NAT router and the LAN router configuration, and then paste it into a WordPad document named LGxxLab9-3.rtf (where xx is the assigned number of your lab group).

   Your instructor will ask you to turn it in at the end of the lab.

8. Leave the console open for the next exercise.

## EXERCISE 9-6: DEMONSTRATING NAT

**Estimated completion time: 20 minutes**

In this exercise, you will test the functionality of your NAT router and use Network Monitor to examine the modifications that NAT makes to network packets.

1. On Computerxx, open a Command Prompt window, and then use the Ping utility to test the computer's connectivity to Server01 and Computeryy, using their IP addresses.

   **QUESTION**   Record the commands you used to perform these tests.

   **QUESTION**   What are the results of the tests?

2. On Computeryy, log on to the LGxx domain (where xx is the number assigned to your lab group by your instructor), using the Administrator account and the password **Pa$$w0rd**.

3. Open a Command Prompt window on Computeryy, type **ping 10.1.100.1** and then press ENTER.

   **QUESTION**   What is the result of this ping test? What does the result demonstrate?

4. On Computerxx, open Network Monitor and configure the program to capture traffic from the Lab Group Network Connection interface.

5. From the Capture menu, select Start to begin capturing traffic.

6. On Computeryy, repeat the ping test you performed in step 3.

7. On Computerxx, from the Capture menu, select Stop And View to end the capture process.

The Capture: # Summary window containing the captured frames appears.

8. In the Capture: # Summary window, locate the ICMP Echo frames you generated with the Ping utility on Computeryy.

> **QUESTION** What is the destination IP address of the ICMP Echo frames (as displayed in the Dst Other Addr column)?

> **QUESTION** What is the source IP address of the ICMP Echo frames?

9. Locate the ICMP Echo Reply frames sent in response to the Echo frames.

> **QUESTION** What are the source and destination IP addresses for the Echo Reply frames?

> **QUESTION** How has the reconfiguration of RRAS from a LAN router to a NAT router affected these captures?

10. Minimize the Capture: # Summary window in Network Monitor, and then reconfigure the program to capture traffic from the Classroom Network Connection interface.

11. Start the capture process on Computerxx and repeat the ping test you performed in step 3 on Computeryy.

**12.** Display the results of your capture on Computer*xx* and write the source and destination IP addresses of the Echo and Echo Reply frames in the following table.

|  | Source IP Address | Destination IP Address |
| --- | --- | --- |
| **ICMP Echo** |  |  |
| **ICMP Echo Reply** |  |  |

> **QUESTION**   How do these results differ from those you captured on the Lab Group Network Connection interface?

> **QUESTION**   How has the reconfiguration of RRAS from a LAN router to a NAT router affected these captures?

**13.** On Computer*yy*, open Internet Explorer, type **http://10.1.100.1** in the Address message box, and then press ENTER.

> **QUESTION**   What happens?

**14.** On Computer*xx*, in the Routing And Remote Access console, select the NAT/Basic Firewall icon in the scope pane. Then in the details pane, select the Classroom Network Connection entry, and then select Show Mappings from the Action menu.

The COMPUTER*xx* – Network Address Translation Session Mapping Table appears.

> **QUESTION**   How did NAT use the information in this table to modify the TCP frames you just created by accessing the Web server on Server01?

**15.** Take a screen shot (using ALT+PRNT SCRN) of the Routing And Remote Access console showing the COMPUTER*xx* – Network Address Translation Session Mapping Table, and then paste it into a WordPad document named LG*xx*Lab09-4.rtf (where *xx* is the assigned number of your lab group).

Your instructor will ask you to turn it in at the end of the lab.

**16.** Close the Routing And Remote Access console.

# LAB REVIEW QUESTIONS

**Estimated completion time: 15 minutes**

1. When you create packet filters in RRAS, you can choose to filter inbound or outbound traffic for each of the available network interfaces. In Exercise 9-3 you created a packet filter in the Outbound Filters dialog box of the Lab Group Network Connection interface. For each of the three following alternatives, specify whether creating the exact same filter would be as effective as the one you created in the lab and state why or why not.

    a. The Inbound Filters dialog box of the Lab Group Network Connection interface

    b. The Outbound Filters dialog box of the Classroom Network Connection interface

    c. The Inbound Filters dialog box of the Classroom Network Connection interface

2. With RRAS configured as in Exercise 9-3, if you create an outbound filter on the Lab Group Network Connection interface specifying the TCP protocol and port number 25, which of the following tasks would computers on the lab group network be unable to perform? (Choose all answers that are correct.)

    a. Send outgoing e-mail messages to Simple Mail Transfer Protocol (SMTP) servers on the Internet

    b. Run an SMTP server on the lab group network

    c. Retrieve incoming e-mail from Post Office Protocol 3 (POP3) servers on the Internet

    d. Run a POP3 server on the lab group network

3. How does the basic firewall mechanism provided with the NAT implementation of Windows Server 2003 protect the private network?

4. Why must a NAT router used to provide secure access to the Internet have a registered IP address?

## LAB CHALLENGE 9-1: REVERSING THE NAT CONFIGURATION

**Estimated completion time: 20 minutes**

1. On your lab group Computer*xx*, reset RRAS as you did in Exercise 9-4, and then reconfigure the service as described in Exercise 9-5, but this time reverse the NAT configuration by selecting Lab Group Network Connection as the public network interface.

2. From Computer*yy*, attempt to ping the Server01 IP address 10.1.100.1.

   **QUESTION**    Why is this ping test unsuccessful?

   **QUESTION**    What adjustment can you make in the current RRAS configuration on Computer*xx* to modify the results of the ping test?

3. Take a screen shot (using ALT+PRNT SCRN) of the Routing And Remote Access console, showing the parameter you must adjust to enable the ping test to succeed, and then paste it into a WordPad document named LG*xx*Lab9-5.rtf (where *xx* is the assigned number of your lab group).

   Your instructor will ask you to turn it in at the end of the lab.

## LAB 10
# REMOTE NETWORK ACCESS

**This lab contains the following exercises and activities:**

- Exercise 10-1: Resetting RRAS

- Exercise 10-2: Configuring a VPN Server

- Exercise 10-3: Configuring a VPN Client

- Exercise 10-4: Establishing a VPN Connection

- Exercise 10-5: Analyzing VPN Traffic

- Exercise 10-6: Reconfiguring RRAS

- Lab Review Questions

- Lab Challenge 10-1: Configuring a VPN Server Manually

## BEFORE YOU BEGIN

To complete this lab, you will need to obtain the following materials from your instructor:

- The two-digit number assigned to your lab group. This number forms the name of your lab group (LG*xx*, where *xx* is the number assigned to your group).

- Table 6-1 from Lab 6 of this manual, in which you added the Transmission Control Protocol/Internet Protocol (TCP/IP) configuration parameters you computed for your lab group network.

**After completing this lab, you will be able to:**

- Configure the Routing and Remote Access Service (RRAS) on a computer running Microsoft Windows Server 2003 to function as a virtual private network (VPN) server.

- Configure a computer running Microsoft Windows to function as a VPN client.

- Establish a VPN connection and analyze the traffic it generates.

**Estimated lesson time:   120 minutes**

## SCENARIO

The Research and Development (R&D) department at Contoso, Ltd. is building a field research station at a remote location, where scientists will gather data to send back to the R&D network at Contoso's home office. Because this data is highly sensitive and must be secured, you decide to set up a VPN server on the company network. The users at the research station can connect to the VPN server and send their data securely.

## EXERCISE 10-1: RESETTING RRAS

**Estimated completion time: 5 minutes**

In this exercise you will remove the RRAS configuration, just as you did in Exercise 9-4 in Lab 9 of this manual.

1. Log on to Computer*xx* as Administrator, using the password **Pa$$w0rd**.

2. Open the Routing And Remote Access console, click the COMPUTER*xx* icon (where *xx* is the number assigned to your lab group by your instructor), and then select Disable Routing And Remote Access from the Action menu.

   A Routing And Remote Access message box appears, warning that you are about to disable the router.

3. Click Yes.

   RRAS returns to its default unconfigured state.

## EXERCISE 10-2: CONFIGURING A VPN SERVER

**Estimated completion time: 15 minutes**

In this exercise you will configure RRAS on Computer*xx* to function as a remote access server using VPN connections.

1. In the Routing And Remote Access console on Computer*xx*, select Configure And Enable Routing And Remote Access from the Action menu.

   The Routing And Remote Access Server Setup Wizard appears.

2. Click Next to bypass the Welcome page.

The Configuration page appears.

3. Verify that the Remote Access (Dial-Up Or VPN) option is selected, and then click Next.

The Remote Access page appears.

4. Select the VPN check box, and then click Next.

The VPN Connection page appears.

5. In the Network Interfaces list, select Lab Group Network Connection.

For the purposes of this lab, your lab group network will function as the equivalent of an Internet connection between Computer*xx* and Computer*yy*. In a production environment, any computer running Windows that is connected to the Internet can function as a VPN client and connect to a VPN server that is also connected to the Internet.

6. Clear the Enable Security On The Selected Interface By Setting Up Static Packet Filters check box, and then click Next.

The IP Address Assignment page appears.

7. Ensure that the Automatically option is selected, and then click Next.

The Manage Multiple Remote Access Servers page appears.

8. Ensure that the No, Use Routing And Remote Access To Authenticate Connection Requests option is selected, and then click Next.

The Completing The Routing And Remote Access Server Setup Wizard page appears.

9. Click Finish.

A message box appears, informing you of the need for the DHCP Relay Agent.

10. Click OK to continue.

RRAS starts.

> **QUESTION**   How does the Routing And Remote Access console inter-face for the Remote Access configuration differ from that of the Network Address Translation (NAT) router configuration you created in Lab 9?

11. Take a screen shot (using ALT+PRNT SCRN) of the Routing And Remote Access console, and then paste it into a WordPad document named LGxxLab10-1.rtf (where xx is the assigned number of your lab group).

Your instructor will ask you to turn it in at the end of the lab.

12. Leave the Routing And Remote Access console open for a later exercise.

13. Click Start, select Administrative Tools, and then select Active Directory Users And Computers.

The Active Directory Users and Computers console appears.

14. Select the Users container and open the Properties dialog box for the Administrator object.

15. Click the Dial-In tab, select the Allow Access option, and then click OK.

16. Close the Active Directory Users And Computers console.

## EXERCISE 10-3: CONFIGURING A VPN CLIENT

**Estimated completion time: 10 minutes**

In this exercise you will configure your lab group Computeryy to function as a remote access client, using a VPN connection.

1. Log on to your Computeryy with the local Administrator account, using the password **Pa$$w0rd**.

2. Click Start, select Control Panel, right-click Network Connections, and then select Open.

The Network Connections window appears.

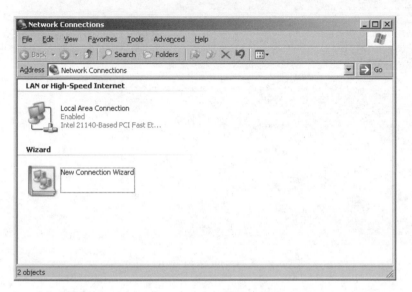

3. Double-click the New Connection Wizard icon.

The Welcome To The New Connection Wizard page appears.

4. Click Next.

The Network Connection Type page appears.

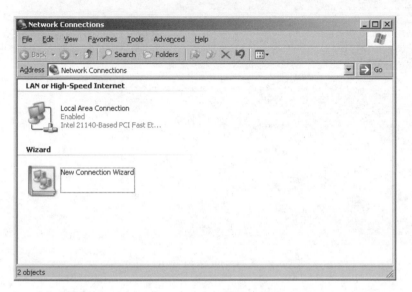

**5.** Select Connect To The Network At My Workplace, and then click Next.

The Network Connection page appears.

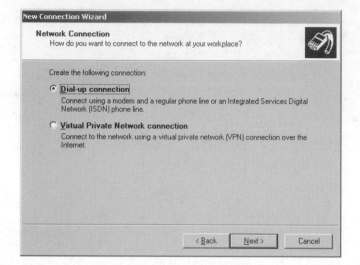

**6.** Select Virtual Private Network Connection, and then click Next.

The Connection Name page appears.

**QUESTION**    If you were to select Dial-Up Connection instead of Virtual Private Network Connection, what additional piece of information would you have to supply later in the configuration process?

**7.** In the Company Name text box, type **Computerxx**, and then click Next.

The VPN Server Selection page appears.

**8.** In the Host Name Or IP Address text box, type the Internet Protocol (IP) address of Computerxx, and then click Next.

> **NOTE   Lab Group IP Addresses**   Consult the information you entered in Table 6-1 from Lab 6 of this manual for Computerxx's IP address.

The Connection Availability page appears.

**9.** Select Anyone's Use, and then click Next.

The Completing The New Connection Wizard page appears.

10. Click Finish.

The Connect Computerxx dialog box appears.

11. Leave the Connect Computerxx dialog box open for the next exercise.

## EXERCISE 10-4: ESTABLISHING A VPN CONNECTION

**Estimated completion time: 15 minutes**

In this exercise you will capture the traffic generated by your lab group computers as they establish a VPN connection.

1. On Computerxx, launch Network Monitor and configure the program to capture traffic from the Lab Group Network Connection interface.

2. From the Capture menu, select Start to begin capturing traffic.

3. On Computeryy, in the Connect Computerxx dialog box, leave Administrator in the User Name text box, type **Pa$$w0rd** in the Password text box, and then click Connect.

**QUESTION**  What happens?

4. Click Accept.

A connection is established to RRAS on Computerxx.

5. Click the Computerxx icon in the taskbar.

   The Computerxx Status dialog box appears.

6. Click the Details tab.

> **QUESTION**   What authentication protocol did Computeryy use to con-
> nect to Computerxx?

> **QUESTION**   What encryption protocol is the connection using?

7. Take a screen shot (using ALT+PRNT SCRN) of the Computerxx Status
   dialog box, and then paste it into a WordPad document named
   LGxxLab10-2.rtf (where xx is the assigned number of your lab group).

   Your instructor will ask you to turn it in at the end of the lab.

8. Close the Computerxx Status dialog box.

9. On Computerxx, in the scope pane of the Routing And Remote Access
   console, click the Remote Access Clients icon.

10. Double-click the entry in the details pane.

    The Status dialog box appears.

11. Take a screen shot of the Status dialog box, and then paste it into a
    WordPad document named LGxxLab10-3.rtf.

    Your instructor will ask you to turn it in at the end of the lab.

12. Close the Status dialog box.

# EXERCISE 10-5: ANALYZING VPN TRAFFIC

**Estimated completion time: 20 minutes**

In this exercise you will examine the Point-to-Point Tunneling Protocol (PPTP)
and Point-to-Point Protocol (PPP) traffic generated during the VPN connection
establishment process.

1. In Network Monitor on Computerxx, select Stop And View from the
   Capture menu.

   A Capture: # Summary window appears.

**2.** Locate the first PPTP packet in the capture summary and double-click it to display the Detail and Hex panes containing the packet's contents.

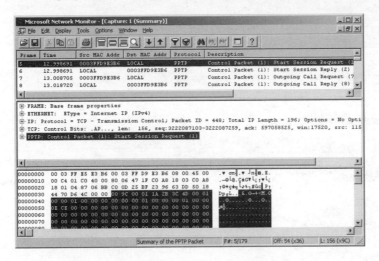

**QUESTION**   What transport layer protocol is carrying the PPTP messages?

**3.** Create a display filter in Network Monitor that causes the application to display only the frames containing PPP information.

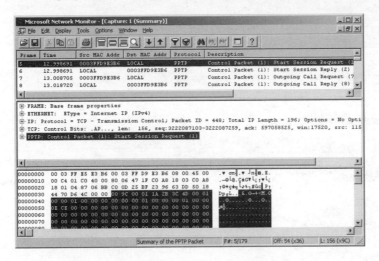

**4.** Select the first frame in the filtered traffic sample.

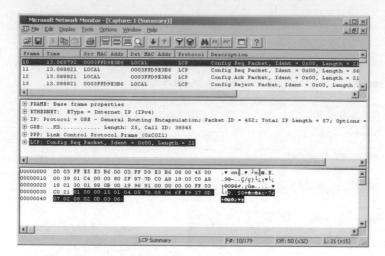

> **QUESTION**   What is the primary protocol in this frame (that is, what abbreviation appears in the Summary pane's Protocol column)?

> **QUESTION**   What is the full name of this protocol? What is its usual function?

**5.** Examine the information in the Detail pane.

> **QUESTION**   List all the protocols used to create the frame, from the bottom of the Open Systems Interconnection (OSI) reference model to the top.

> **QUESTION**   What is the maximum receive unit (MRU) value suggested by this frame? How can you tell?

**6.** Scroll down in the Summary pane and examine all of the frames displayed there.

> **QUESTION**   List the primary protocols used by the frames in this filtered traffic sample and explain the function of each one in the PPP connection establishment process.

**7.** Scroll to the bottom of the Summary pane and examine one of the frames with PPP as its primary protocol.

> **QUESTION**   Why can't you see what protocols are encapsulated within the PPP frame?

8. Close Network Monitor and don't save the capture.

# EXERCISE 10-6: RECONFIGURING RRAS

**Estimated completion time: 10 minutes**

In this exercise you will reset RRAS to the basic local area network (LAN) router configuration you created in Lab 7 of this manual.

1. On Computerxx, open the Routing And Remote Access console.

2. Reset RRAS to its unconfigured state, as you did in Exercise 10-1.

3. Reconfigure RRAS to function as a basic LAN router, using the procedure you performed in Exercise 7-3 in Lab 7 of this manual.

# LAB REVIEW QUESTIONS

**Estimated completion time: 15 minutes**

1. In Exercise 10-4, why was Computeryy unable to establish a connection with Computerxx using IPX?

2. Judging solely from the information in the Detail pane, at what layer of the OSI reference model is PPTP operating? How do you know?

3. In Exercise 10-5, you listed the protocols that made up the protocol stack in a captured PPP frame. What was unusual about the order of the protocols in this frame?

4. How can you explain the unusual protocol encapsulation arrangement you observed in Exercise 10-5?

## LAB CHALLENGE 10-1: CONFIGURING A VPN SERVER MANUALLY

**Estimated completion time: 30 minutes**

When you set up RRAS on a computer running Windows Server 2003, the options you can select on the Configuration page of the Routing And Remote Access Server Setup Wizard differ only in the default settings for the service's parameters. Once you set up the service using one configuration, you can switch to another without having to erase the existing parameter settings.

To complete this challenge, do the following:

1. Use the Routing And Remote Access console on Computerxx to modify the standard LAN router configuration you restored in Exercise 10-6, into the VPN remote access configuration you created in Exercise 10-2.

   Do not select Disable Routing And Remote Access to delete the existing RRAS configuration. Instead, modify the existing configuration using the Properties dialog boxes available in the console.

2. Write a procedure detailing the modifications you make to the configuration.

3. Demonstrate your success by connecting to RRAS on Computerxx from the VPN client you created on Computeryy in Exercise 10-3.

## POST-LAB CLEANUP

1. On Computerxx, open the Routing And Remote Access console.

2. Reset RRAS to its unconfigured state, as you did in Exercise 10-1.

3. Reconfigure RRAS to function as a basic LAN router, using the procedure you performed in Exercise 7-3 in Lab 7 of this manual.

## TROUBLESHOOTING LAB C:

# TROUBLESHOOTING NAT AND VPNS

Troubleshooting Lab C is a practical application of the knowledge you have acquired from Labs 1 through 10. Your instructor or lab assistant has changed your computer configuration, causing it to "break." Your task in this lab will be to apply your acquired skills to troubleshoot and resolve the break. Two scenarios are presented that lay out the parameters of the breaks and the conditions that must be met for the scenarios to be resolved. The first break scenario involves troubleshooting Network Address Translation (NAT), and the second break scenario involves troubleshooting a virtual private network (VPN) connection.

**CAUTION**   Do not proceed with this lab until you receive guidance from your instructor.

Your instructor will inform you which break scenario you will be performing (Break Scenario 1 or Break Scenario 2) and which computer to use. Your instructor or lab assistant might also have special instructions. Consult with your instructor before proceeding.

## Break Scenario 1

Howard is the owner of Tailspin Toys, a small company with a 25-node network consisting of one server running Microsoft Windows Server 2003 and 24 workstations. Howard wants to provide his employees with Internet access, but his two major concerns are keeping costs low and protecting his network from Internet intruders. As a result, Howard has decided to use Routing and Remote Access Service (RRAS) on his Windows Server 2003 server as a NAT server.

The NAT server is called Computer*xx* and has two network interfaces. The Classroom Network Connection interface is connected to the Internet, and the Lab Group Network Connection interface is connected to the local area network (LAN) with the 24 workstations, one of which is called Computer*yy*. After configuring RRAS on Computer*xx*, Howard logs on to Computer*yy* and attempts to access the Internet by pinging his Internet router, which has the Internet Protocol

(IP) address 10.1.100.1. The attempt fails and Howard can't access the Internet from Computeryy. Finally, he calls you, a network consultant, to come out and resolve the problem. Troubleshoot Computerxx until you can ping the 10.1.100.1 address from Computeryy using NAT.

As you resolve the problem, fill out the worksheet in the Lab Manual\Trouble-shootingLabC folder and include the following information:

- A description of the problem

- A list of all steps taken to diagnose the problem, even the ones that didn't work

- A description of the exact issue and solution

- A list of the tools and resources you used to help solve this problem

## Break Scenario 2

Mark Lee is attempting to telecommute from home for the first time, using a VPN connection. His employer, Blue Yonder Airlines, has a VPN server installed on a Windows Server 2003 computer called Computerxx, and the network administrator has created an account for Mark using the logon name **mlee** with the password **Pa$$w0rd**. Mark has created a VPN client connection on his home computer, which is called Computeryy, but he is unable to connect to the server at the Blue Yonder office. The company has sent you out to Mark's home to get him connected to the company network. Troubleshoot the computers until Mark can connect to the server using a VPN connection.

As you resolve the problem, fill out the worksheet in the Lab Manual\Trouble-shootingLabC folder and include the following information:

- A description of the problem

- A list of all steps taken to diagnose the problem, even the ones that didn't work

- A description of the exact issue and solution

- A list of the tools and resources you used to help solve this problem

# NETWORK TROUBLESHOOTING TOOLS

**This lab contains the following exercises and activities:**

- Exercise 11-1: Using Windows System Monitor

- Exercise 11-2: Creating a Counter Log

- Exercise 11-3: Viewing a Counter Log

- Exercise 11-4: Creating a Performance Alert

- Exercise 11-5: Using Tracert.exe

- Exercise 11-6: Using Nslookup.exe

- Lab Review Questions

- Lab Challenge 11-1. Linux Performance Monitoring

## BEFORE YOU BEGIN

To complete this lab, you will need to obtain the following materials from your instructor:

- The two-digit number assigned to your lab group. This number is used in the name of your lab group (LG*xx*, where *xx* is the number assigned to your group).

- Table 6-1 from Lab 6 of this manual, which contains the Transmission Control Protocol/Internet Protocol (TCP/IP) configuration parameters you computed for your lab group network.

- The Internet Protocol (IP) address of the Computer*yy* computer in one of the other student lab groups in the classroom.

To complete the exercises in this lab, the Routing and Remote Access Service (RRAS) on Computer*xx* must be set to the standard local area network (LAN) routing configuration, with Routing Information Protocol (RIP) installed, which you first created in Lab 7 of this manual and which you restored in Exercise 10-6 in Lab 10 of this manual.

**After completing this lab, you will be able to:**

■ View information about a computer running Microsoft Windows in real time, using System Monitor.

■ Create a system baseline counter log, using the Microsoft Windows Server 2003 Performance console.

■ Create an alert that triggers an action when system performance passes a specified threshold.

■ Use the Ping, Traceroute, and Nslookup utilities on a computer running Windows.

**Estimated lesson time:   135 minutes**

## SCENARIO

As the new network administrator for Contoso, Ltd., you are currently creating a comprehensive performance monitoring plan for the company network. As part of this plan, you must compile baseline performance statistics for the company servers and create a series of alerts that will notify you when conditions reach specific thresholds.

## EXERCISE 11-1: USING WINDOWS SYSTEM MONITOR

**Estimated completion time: 15 minutes**
In this exercise you will use the System Monitor in the Windows Server 2003 Performance console to view performance levels on Computeryy.

1. Log on to Computeryy using the local Administrator account, using the password **Pa$$w0rd.**

2. Click Start, select Administrative Tools, and then select Performance.

   The Performance console appears, with the default System Monitor snap-in displayed.

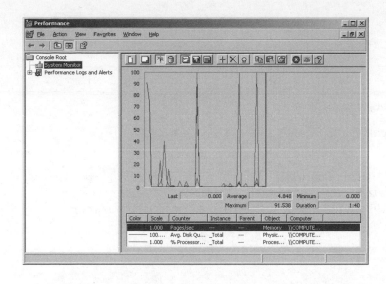

QUESTION    What counters appear in the System Monitor display by default?

3. Remove the three default counters from the System Monitor graph by selecting each one in the legend in turn and clicking Delete.

4. Click the Add button on the toolbar.

The Add Counters dialog box appears.

5. In the Performance Object drop-down list, select System.

6. In the Select Counters From List box, select Processor Queue Length, and then click Add.

QUESTION    What happens?

7. Using the same process, add the following counters to the graph:

❑ Server Work Queues(0): Queue Length

❑ Memory: Page Faults/Sec

❑ Memory: Pages/Sec

❑ PhysicalDisk (_Total): Current Disk Queue Length

> **NOTE   Using Counters**   Each of the counters specified in this lab is notated using a performance object, an instance enclosed in parentheses (where applicable), and a performance counter.

8. Click Close to close the Add Counters dialog box.

> **QUESTION**   Does this selection of counters make for an effective graph? Why or why not?

9. Click Properties.

The System Monitor Properties dialog box appears.

10. Click the Graph tab, and then in the Vertical Scale box, change the value of the Maximum field to 40, and then click OK.

> **QUESTION**   Does this modification make the graph easier or more difficult to read? Why?

11. Take a screen shot (using ALT+PRNT SCRN) of the Performance console and paste it into a WordPad document named LGxxLab11-1.rtf (where *xx* is the assigned number of your lab group).

    Your instructor will ask you to turn it in at the end of the lab.

12. From the console's Window menu, select New Window.

    A new Console Root window appears in the console.

13. In the new Console Root window, click System Monitor in the scope pane and then click Add.

14. Add the following counters to the new System Monitor graph:

    ❑ Network Interface (select the instance for the network interface adapter in the computer): Packets/Sec

    ❑ Network Interface (select the instance for the network interface adapter in the computer): Output Queue Length

    ❑ Server: Bytes Total/Sec

    > **QUESTION**   *Does this selection of counters make for an effective graph? Why or why not?*

15. Take a screen shot (using ALT+PRNT SCRN) of the Performance console and paste it into a WordPad document named LGxxLab11-2.rtf.

    Your instructor will ask you to turn it in at the end of the lab.

16. Leave the Performance console open for a later exercise.

## EXERCISE 11-2: CREATING A COUNTER LOG

**Estimated completion time: 15 minutes**

In this exercise you will use the Performance console to create counter logs documenting the performance of the server under normal operating conditions. If problems arise with the server later, you can compare the system's current performance levels with the baseline levels established here.

1. Log on to Computerxx as Administrator, using the password **Pa$$w0rd**.

2. Open the Performance console and, in the scope pane, expand the Performance Logs And Alerts icon, and then select Counter Logs.

**3.** From the Action menu, select New Log Settings.

The New Log Settings dialog box appears.

**4.** In the Name text box, type **Computerxx Baseline** and then click OK.

The Computerxx Baseline dialog box appears.

**5.** Click Add Counters.

The Add Counters dialog box appears.

**6.** Using the same procedure you used to add counters to the System Monitor graph in Exercise 11-1, add the following counters:

❑ Processor (_Total): % Processor Time

❑ Processor (_Total): Interrupts/Sec

❑ System: Processor Queue Length

❑ Server Work Queues (0): Queue Length

❑ Memory: Available Bytes

❑ Memory: Committed Bytes

❑ Memory: Page Faults/Sec

❑   Memory: Pages/Sec

❑   Memory: Pool Nonpaged Bytes

❑   PhysicalDisk (_Total): % Disk Time

❑   PhysicalDisk (_Total): Avg. Disk Bytes/Transfer

❑   PhysicalDisk (_Total): Current Disk Queue Length

❑   PhysicalDisk (_Total): Disk Bytes/sec

❑   LogicalDisk (_Total): % Free Space

❑   Network Interface (select the All Instances option): Bytes Total/Sec

❑   Network Interface (select the All Instances option): Output Queue Length

❑   Server: Bytes Total/Sec

7. Click Close.

8. Set the Interval value to 10 and the Units value to Seconds.

9. In the Run As text box, type **Administrator**.

10. Click Set Password.

The Set Password dialog box appears.

11. Type **Pa$$w0rd** in the Password and Confirm Password message boxes, and then click OK.

12. Click the Log Files tab.

13. Change the value of the End File Names With field to yyyymmdd.

**QUESTION** What will be the exact name of the counter log you are about to create? How can you tell?

**14.** Click the Schedule tab.

**15.** In the Start Log box, select the Manually (Using The Shortcut Menu) option.

**16.** In the Stop Log box, select the After option and set the interval to 5 Minutes.

For the purposes of this lab exercise, you are configuring the counter log to capture data for 5 minutes. On a production server, your baseline log should run for at least several hours.

**17.** Click OK.

A Computer*xx* Baseline message box appears, asking if you want to create the C:\Perflogs folder, the default location for the counter log files.

**18.** Click Yes.

**QUESTION** What happens?

**19.** Take a screen shot (using ALT+PRNT SCRN) of the Performance console and paste it into a WordPad document named LG*xx*Lab11-3.rtf (where *xx* is the assigned number of your lab group).

Your instructor will ask you to turn it in at the end of the lab.

**20.** Select the Baseline counter log you just created, and then select Start from the Action menu.

The icon for the counter log changes from red to green, indicating that the log is running.

**21.** Leave the Performance console open for the next exercise.

# EXERCISE 11-3: VIEWING A COUNTER LOG

**Estimated completion time: 15 minutes**

In this exercise you will view the contents of the counter log you created in Exercise 11-2.

**1.** Wait until 5 minutes have elapsed since you started the Computer*xx* Baseline counter log you created in Exercise 11-2 and refresh the display.

**QUESTION**   What happens?

**2.** In the scope pane, select System Monitor, and then click the New Counter Set button on the toolbar.

**3.** Click the View Log Data button on the toolbar.

The System Monitor Properties dialog box appears.

4. Select Log Files, click Add, browse to the C:\Perflogs folder, and then select the Computer*xx* Baseline_*yyyymmdd*.blg file (where *yyyymmdd* is the current date). Click Open.

5. Click the Data tab, and then click Add.

   The Add Counters dialog box appears.

6. For each performance object, select All Counters and All Instances, and then click Add. Click Close when you've selected all performance objects.

7. Click OK to close the System Monitor Properties dialog box.

   The log information appears in the System Monitor graph.

8. Take a screen shot (using ALT+PRNT SCRN) of the Performance console and paste it into a WordPad document named LG*xx*Lab11-4.rtf (where *xx* is the assigned number of your lab group).

   Your instructor will ask you to turn it in at the end of the lab.

9. Leave the Performance console open for the next exercise.

## EXERCISE 11-4: CREATING A PERFORMANCE ALERT

**Estimated completion time: 15 minutes**

In this exercise you will use the Performance console to create an alert that warns you when network traffic exceeds a certain level.

1. On Computer*yy*, in the Performance console's scope pane, expand the Performance Logs And Alerts icon, and then select Alerts.

2. From the Action menu, select New Alert Settings.

   The New Alert Settings dialog box appears.

3. In the Name text box, type **Network Traffic** and then click OK.

   The Network Traffic dialog box appears.

4. Click Add.

   The Add Counters dialog box appears.

5. Add the Network Interface: Bytes Total/Sec counter, and then click Close.

6. Set the Alert When The Value Is field to Over, and then set the Limit field to 10000.

7. Set the Sample Data Every field to 30 Seconds.

8. In the Run As text box, type **Administrator** and then click Set Password to specify the password for the Administrator account.

9. Click the Action tab.

10. Select the Send A Network Message To check box and type **Computeryy** in the text box.

11. Click the Schedule tab.

12. In the Start Scan box, select the Manually option.

13. In the Stop Scan box, select After 30 Minutes, and then click OK.

    The Network Traffic alert appears in the details pane.

14. Take a screen shot (using ALT+PRNT SCRN) of the Performance console and paste it into a WordPad document named LG*xx*Lab11-5.rtf (where *xx* is the assigned number of your lab group).

    Your instructor will ask you to turn it in at the end of the lab.

15. Select the Network Traffic alert you just created, and then select Start from the Action menu.

    The icon for the Network Traffic alert changes from red to green, indicating that scanning has begun.

16. Open a Command Prompt window on Computeryy and use the Ping utility to generate network traffic with a command like the following: **ping ipaddress −t −l 65500** (where *ipaddress* is the address of Computer*xx*'s Lab Group Network Connection interface).

17. Allow the Ping program to run for 1 minute, and then press CTRL+C to stop it.

**QUESTION**   What happens as a result of the ping messages?

18. Click Start, select Administrative Tools, and then select Services.

    The Services console appears.

19. In the details pane, select the Messenger service, and then select Properties from the Action menu.

The Messenger Properties dialog box appears.

**20.** Set the Startup Type to Automatic, and then click Apply.

**21.** Click Start to start the service, and then click OK.

**22.** Close the Services console.

**23.** Return to the Command Prompt window and run the same Ping command again for 1 minute.

**QUESTION** What happens now?

**24.** Click OK to close the message box and press CTRL+C to stop the Ping program in the Command Prompt window.

**25.** In the Performance console, select Stop from the Action menu to stop the alert scanning process.

**26.** Close the Performance console.

# EXERCISE 11-5: USING TRACERT.EXE

**Estimated completion time: 15 minutes**

In this exercise you will use Network Monitor to examine the traffic generated by the Windows Ping.exe and Tracert.exe programs.

**1.** Obtain the IP address of the Computeryy computer in one of the other student lab groups in the classroom.

**2.** On Computerxx, launch Network Monitor and configure the program to capture traffic from the Lab Group Network Connection interface.

3. From the Capture menu, select Start to begin capturing frames.

4. On Computeryy, open a Command Prompt window and type **ping** **ipaddress** (where *ipaddress* is the IP address for the Computeryy computer from the other lab group).

> **QUESTION**   What is the result?

5. In the Command Prompt window, type **tracert** *ipaddress*.

> **QUESTION**   What is the result?

6. Take a screen shot (using ALT+PRNT SCRN) of the Command Prompt window, and then paste it into a WordPad document named LGxxLab11-6.rtf (where *xx* is the assigned number of your lab group).

   Your instructor will ask you to turn it in at the end of the lab.

7. In Network Monitor on Computerxx, select Stop And View from the Capture menu.

   The Capture: # Summary window appears.

8. Create a display filter that configures Network Monitor to show only the Internet Control Message Protocol (ICMP) traffic in your captured sample.

9. Take a screen shot of the Network Monitor window, and then paste it into a WordPad document named LGxxLab11-7.rtf.

   Your instructor will ask you to turn it in at the end of the lab.

10. Double-click the first frame with ICMP in the Protocol column.

    The window splits into Summary, Detail, and Hex panes.

11. In the Detail pane, expand the IP heading.

> **QUESTION**   What is the value of the IP: Time To Live field for this frame?

12. In the Detail pane, expand the ICMP heading.

> **QUESTION**   What is the value of the ICMP: Sequence Number field?

13. In the Summary pane, select the next ICMP message.

**QUESTION**   What is the value of the IP: Time To Live field for this frame?

**QUESTION**   What is the value of this frame's ICMP: Sequence Number field?

**QUESTION**   What is the function of this frame? How can you tell for certain?

**QUESTION**   Why don't the two frames have the same TTL value?

**QUESTION**   Based on this information, what program generated these two ICMP messages? How can you tell?

14. Locate the first ICMP frame with Time Exceeded in the Description field, and then select the ICMP Echo message referenced in the See Frame <frame number> part of the description and examine its contents.

**QUESTION**   What is the value of the IP: Time To Live field in the Echo message?

**QUESTION**   How does this value explain the Time Exceeded message that follows?

**QUESTION**   Based on this information, what program generated these two ICMP messages? How can you tell?

15. Close Network Monitor.

# EXERCISE 11-6: USING NSLOOKUP.EXE

**Estimated completion time: 15 minutes**

In this exercise you will use the Nslookup.exe program to access Domain Name System (DNS) information on servers throughout your classroom network.

1. On Computeryy, open a Command Prompt window.

2. At the command prompt, type **nslookup computerxx**, and then press ENTER.

**QUESTION**   What is the result?

3. Take a screen shot (using ALT+PRNT SCRN) of the Command Prompt window showing the successful Nslookup command, and then paste it into a WordPad document named LG*xx*Lab11-8.rtf.

Your instructor will ask you to turn it in at the end of the lab.

**QUESTION**   What DNS server did Nslookup use to resolve the name? How can you tell?

4. At the command prompt, type **nslookup server01** and then press ENTER.

**QUESTION**   Why did Nslookup fail to resolve the name?

5. At the command prompt, type **nslookup server01.contoso.com** and then press ENTER.

**QUESTION**   What is the result now? Why?

6. At the command prompt, type **nslookup server01 10.1.100.1** and then press ENTER.

7. Take a screen shot of the Command Prompt window showing the successful Nslookup command, and then paste it into a WordPad document named LG*xx*Lab11-9.rtf.

Your instructor will ask you to turn it in at the end of the lab.

**QUESTION**   Why was this attempt to resolve the name successful?

8. At the command prompt, type **nslookup** and then press ENTER.

A new prompt appears, consisting only of a right angle bracket (>).

9. At the prompt, type **computer*xx*** and then press ENTER.

**QUESTION**   What happens?

10. At the prompt, type **server01** and then press ENTER.

**QUESTION**   Why does the name resolution fail?

11. At the command prompt, type **server 10.1.100.1** and then press ENTER; then type **server01** and press ENTER.

> **QUESTION**   Why is the name resolution successful this time?

12. Type **exit** at the prompt, and then press ENTER to return to the standard command prompt.

13. Close the Command Prompt window.

## LAB REVIEW QUESTIONS

**Estimated completion time: 15 minutes**

1. Under what circumstances would a counter log fail to function properly if you did not supply an account name and password in the Run As parameter?

2. Based on the frames you captured in Exercise 11-5, how many ICMP Echo messages does Tracert send with each Time To Live value?

3. How does the Add Counters dialog box you saw in Exercise 11-3 differ from the ones you used in Exercise 11-1 and Exercise 11-2?

4. What are the functions of the −t and −l parameters you used in the Ping command line in Exercise 11-4?

5. In Exercise 11-5, what happens when the Tracert program on Computeryy starts sending ICMP Echo messages with an IP: Time To Live value of 3?

6. In Exercise 11-6, why did Nslookup generate an error stating that it could not find a name for Computer*xx*'s IP address because the domain does not exist? What must you do to enable Nslookup to run without generating this error?

## LAB CHALLENGE 11-1: LINUX PERFORMANCE MONITORING

**Estimated completion time: 30 minutes**

In this challenge you will explore some of the system monitoring capabilities of the Linux operating system by working on your classroom's LinuxServer01 computer.

1. At the LinuxServer01 server, log on as root, using the password supplied by your instructor.

2. Click the Main Menu icon, select System Tools, and then select System Monitor.

3. Based on the information displayed by the System Monitor application, answer the following questions:

> **QUESTION**  What process currently running on the system is using the most memory?

> **QUESTION**  How can you tell?

> **QUESTION**  How much memory is the System Monitor application itself using?

4. Click the Resource Monitor tab and maximize System Monitor.

5. Take a screen shot (using ALT+PRNT SCRN) of System Monitor, and save it to a file called LGxxLab11-10.png (where xx is the assigned number of your lab group).

   Your instructor will ask you to turn it in at the end of the lab.

6. Click the Main Menu icon, select System Tools, and then select System Logs.

7. On the left of System Logs dialog box, click System Log.

8. Create a filter by typing start in the Filter For text box and clicking Filter.

9. Take a screen shot of the window and save it to a file called LGxxLab11-11.png.

   Your instructor will ask you to turn it in at the end of the lab.

10. Open a Terminal window by clicking the Main Menu icon, select System Tools, and then select Terminal.

11. Maximize the Terminal window, type **top** and then press ENTER.

12. Based on the information displayed by the top application, answer the following questions:

> **QUESTION**  How many processes are currently running on the computer?

**QUESTION**   *How much free memory is on the system?*

13. Take a screen shot of the Terminal window containing the top display, and then save it to a file called LG*xx*Lab11-12.png.

    Your instructor will ask you to turn it in at the end of the lab.

14. Press Q to exit the top program.

    Close all open windows and restart the computer.

## LAB 12
# NETWORK TROUBLESHOOTING PROCEDURES

**This lab contains the following exercises and activities:**

- Exercise 12-1: Creating a Network Environment

- Exercise 12-2: Documenting a Network

- Exercise 12-3: Introducing Faults

- Exercise 12-4: Troubleshooting a Network

- Lab Challenge 12-1: Troubleshooting an Undocumented Network

## BEFORE YOU BEGIN

To complete this lab, you will need to obtain the following materials from your instructor:

- The two-digit number assigned to your lab group. This number is used in the name of your group (LG*xx*, where *xx* is the number assigned to your group).

**After completing this lab, you will be able to:**

- Implement a new network configuration.
- Document a network.
- Troubleshoot a network.

**Estimated lesson time: 150 minutes**

# EXERCISE 12-1: CREATING A NETWORK ENVIRONMENT

**Estimated completion time: 20 minutes**

In this exercise you will be responsible for implementing a network environment, using the tools and techniques you have learned about in previous labs. The object will be to create a new network configuration that enables the computers in your lab group to communicate with the classroom servers, as well as all the other lab groups in the classroom. When all the student lab groups in the classroom have completed this exercise, the Computeryy computer in your group should be able to connect to the Computeryy computer in any other group.

Your instructor will give you the details for the networking environment you must create, consisting of the following elements:

- **Network address**   Your instructor will give you a network address that is different from the one you used in Lab 5, Lab 6, and Lab 7 of this manual. Using this network address, you must calculate the Internet Protocol (IP) addresses and subnet mask for the computers on your lab group network and then deploy the addresses in the manner specified by your instructor. You might have to configure the Transmission Control Protocol/Internet Protocol (TCP/IP) settings manually for your lab group computers, or you might have to use the Dynamic Host Configuration Protocol (DHCP) server running on your lab group Computerxx to deploy them.

- **Protocol configuration**   Your instructor will specify what protocol modules you should have installed on your lab group computers and how they should be bound to the network interface adapters in the computers.

- **Router configuration**   For your lab group network to communicate with the rest of the classroom, you must have a functioning router. Your instructor will specify a router configuration for your lab group, including the type of Routing and Remote Access Service (RRAS) configuration you should use, such as local area network (LAN) or Network Address Translation (NAT) routing, and whether you should use dynamic or static routing.

# EXERCISE 12-2: DOCUMENTING A NETWORK

**Estimated completion time: 15 minutes**

After you have finished setting up your network according to your instructor's guidelines, your next task is to document what you have done. Imagine that you are a network administrator leaving a company (under favorable circumstances) and you want to give your successor as much insight into the network configuration as possible. Later, in Exercise 12-4, this document will be the only information given to the students who will troubleshoot your network, so try to provide information you would like to have when troubleshooting their network.

Your document should include the following:

- The domain name, computer names, and passwords for the lab group computers

- The TCP/IP configuration parameters you used and how you assigned them

- The router configuration and the source of the routing table entries

- A network diagram like the one you created in Lab 2 of this manual, with all the components properly labeled

Be sure to put your name on the document you create, because after you give it to the students who will troubleshoot your network, they will submit it to the instructor for evaluation.

# EXERCISE 12-3: INTRODUCING FAULTS

**Estimated completion time: 10 minutes**

For this exercise your instructor will give you one or more modifications for you to make to your lab group network. The modifications will inhibit the network's communications in some way. You might be instructed to modify specific configuration parameters on one or both of your computers, to alter the hardware configuration of your network, or to alter both.

In essence, you are breaking your network so that other students can troubleshoot it. Each lab group will have a different combination of faults so that every student will have a unique troubleshooting experience.

# EXERCISE 12-4: TROUBLESHOOTING A NETWORK

**Estimated completion time: 45 minutes**

In this exercise your instructor will assign you to another lab group network in the classroom. The students in the other lab group have documented their network and introduced specific faults into the network configuration. Given only the documentation supplied by the other students, your job is to test the network, locate the source of the problem, repair it, and document your efforts.

In this exercise the process is more important than the results. You will be evaluated not only on your success or failure in resolving the problem, but also on the procedures you use to detect, diagnose, and fix it. Documentation is crucial. You must keep a detailed journal of the entire troubleshooting process, including information such as the following:

- The steps you took to test the network

- The results of each test

- The communications problem you discovered

- Possible causes of the problem

- The steps you took to determine the cause

- The tools you used to test the network

- The results of each troubleshooting step

- The actual cause of the problem

- The steps you took to resolve the problem

- The results of retesting to confirm the resolution

> **NOTE  Looking at the Big Picture**   As you are troubleshooting your assigned network, keep in mind that communications between your network and the other networks in the classroom will be inhibited by the problems introduced on the other networks as well as on your own. You might not be able to confirm the success of your troubleshooting process until other students have completed theirs. However, if you can successfully connect to the Server01 computer on the classroom network from your lab group Computeryy, your efforts have been successful.

When you have completed the troubleshooting process, demonstrate to your instructor that the computers in the lab group you have been assigned are functioning properly, and then submit both your troubleshooting journal and the documentation supplied by the other students for evaluation. After you have demonstrated the functionality of your network to your instructor, you must then return the network to the exact "broken" condition as when you found it so that someone else can troubleshoot it during the lab challenge.

# LAB CHALLENGE 12-1: TROUBLESHOOTING AN UNDOCUMENTED NETWORK

**Estimated completion time: 60 minutes**

Assume that you are a network administrator starting a new job and you discover that your predecessor has left you no documentation regarding the current configuration of the network. To complete this challenge, you must repeat Exercise 12-4 by troubleshooting a different lab group network in the classroom. The difference in this case is that you are not permitted to use the documentation created by the students originally assigned to that network.

Before you begin the troubleshooting process, you must determine the configuration of the network yourself by examining the state of its hardware and software and then document it as you did for your own lab group network in Exercise 12-3. After you have completed the documentation process, you can proceed to troubleshoot the network, using the same procedures and keeping the same records as you did in Exercise 12-4. As before, when you have completed the troubleshooting process, demonstrate the functionality of the network to your instructor and submit both your network documentation and your troubleshooting log for evaluation.